THE ARAB EXECUTIVE

THE ARAB EXECUTIVE

Farid A. Muna

Foreword by
Kenneth Simmonds

Palgrave Macmillan

ISBN 978-1-349-16412-7   ISBN 978-1-349-16410-3 (eBook)
DOI 10.1007/978-1-349-16410-3

© Farid A. Muna 1980
Foreword © Kenneth Simmonds 1980
Softcover reprint of the hardcover 1st edition 1980

All rights reserved. For information write:
St. Martin's Press, Inc.,
175 Fifth Avenue, New York, NY 10010

First published in the United States of America in 1980

ISBN 978-0-312-04697-2

Library of Congress Cataloging in Publication Data

Muna, Farid A.
The Arab executive

Originally presented as the author's thesis, University of London.
Bibliography: p.
Includes index.
1. Executives – Arab countries. I. Title.
HF5500.3.A65M86   1980   658.4'00917'4927
80-13711
ISBN 978-0-312-04697-2

To Simon Siksek

Contents

	Page
List of Tables and Figures	ix
Foreword by Kenneth Simmonds	xi
A Note on Transliteration	xii
Acknowledgements	xiii

1	**INTRODUCTION**	1
2	**THE ARAB EXECUTIVE AND HIS ENVIRONMENT**	5
	On Being an Arab	6
	The Arab as a Businessman	8
	The Arab as an Executive	9
	Social Structure: a Mosaic	10
	Recent Political and Economic Developments	13
	Emphasis on Nationalism and Tradition	14
	The Creation of the State of Israel	16
	The Discovery and Exploitation of Petroleum	18
	The Arab Trade Union Movement	22
3	**SOCIAL PRESSURES AND THE EXECUTIVE ROLE**	26
	Social Pressures	26
	Socio-cultural Pressures	29
	Pressures from the Business and Social Community	30
	The Executive Role	34
	Role in Community	35
	Role in Organization	39
4	**THE ARAB APPROACH TO DECISION MAKING**	44
	Decision-making Styles	44
	A Decision-making Profile	47
	Variables Affecting Decision Styles	53
	Consultation	58

5	**CONFLICT MANAGEMENT**	63
6	**INTERPERSONAL STYLE**	71
	Rituals and Customs in Conducting Business	71
	Personal Ties and Connections	74
	The Importance of Loyalty	78
	An Open-Door Tradition	80
	A Preference for 'Informality'	83
7	**ATTITUDES TOWARDS TIME AND CHANGE**	88
	Time Orientation	88
	The Value of Time	89
	Time Horizons	91
	The Myth of Fatalism	93
	Attitudes Towards Change	98
	The Context of Change	99
	The Executive's Attitudes	102
	Ambivalence	106
8	**CONCLUSION AND IMPLICATIONS**	113
	The Importance of Environmental Factors	113
	The Executive as a Change Agent	114
	Modernization without Sacrificing Traditions	115
	Implications	116
	I Management Training and Development	117
	II Expatriate Employees and Foreign Businessmen	120
	III Future Research	121

Appendix 1: Methodology and Data Analysis   125
Appendix 2: The Interview Schedule   131

Bibliography   142
Index   149

List of Tables and Figures

TABLES

		Page
3.1	Social pressures as reported by Arab executives	28
3.2	(a) Executive role and organizational size	40
	(b) Executive role and organizational ownership	40
4.1	Comparison between decisional styles employed in this study and those of previous investigators	46
4.2	Distribution of decision styles for each decision by all Arab executives	49
4.3	Distribution of decision styles by executives from each of the six Arab countries	50
4.4	Mean score of executives from each country for all decisions	51
4.5	Mean score of executives for three categories of decisions	52
4.6	Independent variables accounting for the variance in decision-making styles	55
4.7	Distribution of responses by style for three decision categories	58
6.1	Rituals and customs in conducting business	72
6.2	Executives' preference for loyalty and efficiency: (a) employee; (b) immediate subordinate	79
6.3	The open-door tradition	81
6.4	Bypassing the hierarchy	83
7.1	Proverbs on the value of time	90
7.2	Time horizons: investment, planning, training	92
7.3	Events and factors beyond the executive's control	97
7.4	Preventive measures	97
7.5	Attitudes towards technological and social changes	103
7.6	Attitudes towards social changes, by country	103
7.7	Likelihood of occurrence: technological and social changes	105
8.1	The image of expatriates/foreign businessmen as perceived by Arab executives	121

Appendix Tables

A.1	A statistical profile of Arab executives and their organizations	126
A.2	Analysis of variance (organizational decision 6)	129

FIGURES

3.1	The executive and his environment	27
4.1	The power-sharing continuum	47
4.2	Proportion of responses for all decisions by all Arab executives	49
A.1	Pearson correlation matrix (7 decisions)	128

Foreword

Western managerial awareness of the Arab world jumped sharply with the oil boom of the early 1970s. Up to that time few international businessmen had had direct dealings with Arab executives, and the demand for more background by those anxious to capitalize on the new opportunities brought forth a torrent of writings. At the worst extreme, some texts depicted a caricature of Arab managerial behaviour as an unbounded fatalism apparently unconcerned with rational economic considerations. These alarming generalizations seemed to rest on no more substantial evidence than that Arabic speakers make frequent recourse to *'inshā' Allāh'* (God willing or if God wills). Such caricatures are not only wrong but also quite unbelievable to those from English-speaking cultures with their own common supplications of 'Goodbye' and 'Godspeed', and bold but forgotten proclamations on their coinage of 'Defender of the Faith', and 'In God We Trust'.

Dr Muna guides us away from these trite levels of observation. He has made a determined effort to describe what leading Arab executives think, feel and do within the current environment and given the social pressures placed upon them. Himself an Arab, yet equally at home in the United States and England, Dr Muna has depicted the variety and depth of differences that can exist. It is this sort of picture that the international manager needs if he is to adjust his business practices in ways that really work.

Professor of International Business, *Kenneth Simmonds*
London Business School,
University of London

A Note on Transliteration

The system of transliteration of Arabic words used in most scholarly literature has been followed in this book. Familiar names, however, were not transliterated in this way; instead, they were kept in their simplified form of transliteration. Thus, for example, we have used Quran instead of Qur'ān; King Faisal instead of Faysal; and, of course, the simple transliterations chosen by authors and executives for their names were retained.

Acknowledgements

This book was originally written as a Ph.D. thesis at the London Business School, University of London. The valuable advice, guidance, and assistance of a great number of people made the book possible. To them all I am deeply grateful.

Two persons deserve special acknowledgements: Professor Kenneth Simmonds of the London Business School, and Mr Simon Siksek of the Middle East Industrial Relations Counselors (MEIRC). Professor Simmonds' wealth of knowledge and experience proved invaluable throughout this study. I am indebted to him for his continuous encouragement and support, and above all, for his efforts at directing my work towards the investigation of pragmatic problems. Mr Siksek, to whom the book is dedicated, encouraged me to enter this field and was always willing to take the time needed to discuss my approach and findings. I was also able to draw on his personal experiences as an Arab executive and as a leader in his field.

A number of my colleagues at the London Business School were particularly generous in extending to me needed advice and assistance. They include Drs Dennis Bumstead, Tom Poynter, and Eric Walton. Mr Michael Jefferson of Shell International, London, took a personal interest in my work and offered valuable comments.

In the field, I am indebted to the fifty-two top Arab executives whose patient and in-depth answers to a long list of questions made this study possible. To the thirteen executives who preferred to remain anonymous and to those who allowed me to mention their names herein, I offer my deepest gratitude. I sincerely hope that I will be permitted the opportunity in the future to reciprocate their exceptionally valuable help and cooperation.

Egypt: Mr Mohamed G. Abdel-Hamid
            Dr Adel T. Gazarin
            Mr Mohamed El-Haddad
            Mr W. H. Hegazy
            Mr Yehia Omar

ACKNOWLEDGEMENTS

                Mr Hussein Reda
                Mr Youssef M. Youssef

Jordan: Mr Raouf S. Abujaber
                Mr Tawfiq Kawar
                Mr Bassam R. Mufleh
                Mr Elia C. Nuqul
                Mr Farid Sa'd
                Mr S. K. Tell
                Dr Sobhy A. Tieby

Kuwait: Mr Kutayba Alghanim
                Mr Abdulmalek M. Gharabally
                Mr K. A. Khalaf
                Mr Yousuf M. Al-Nisf
                Mr Fawzi Musaad Al-Saleh
                Mr Abdul Aziz M. Al-Shaya
                Mr Abdul Rahman Al-Sultan

Lebanon: Mr Samir Hamzah
                Mr Said T. Khoury

Saudi Arabia: Mr Omar A. Aggad
                Mr Faysal Al-Bassam
                Mr Adnan M. Khashoggi
                Sheikh Hassan Mishari
                Mr Ali I. Naimi
                Mr Khaled A. Al-Rabiah
                Mr Nasser M. Al-Saleh
                Mr Abdul Aziz Bin Ahmad Al-Sudairy
                Sheikh Abdul Majid Zahid
                Mr Abdulaziz Al-Zamil

UAE: Mr Hussain Abdul-Rehman (Khan Saheb)
                Mr Edward Elias
                Mr Rashed M. Fakhro
                Mr Saif Ahmed Al-Ghurair
                Mr Amal Hourani
                Mr Fadhel M. Khan

Interviewing top executives in six Arab countries required the help of many friends and relatives. I am grateful to Mr Ibrahim Aghabi in Jordan; Mr Saba Abdo and his staff at Dar Al

Handasah, and Mr Adel Shoeib in Egypt; Messrs Faysal Al-Bassam, Paul J. Nance, Ibrahim and Abdullah Yunis in Saudi Arabia; and Mr Mitri Al-Muna in Kuwait.

Also my thanks go to all the expatriates as well as to the persons who participated in the pilot study. Special appreciation for the time and helpful comments kindly given by Dr Hamed Ammar, Messrs Albert Hazbun, Nayef Al-Jaabari, and Mahmud Takieddine.

My colleagues at MEIRC extended to me every help and support throughout the study. In particular, thanks are due to Mr Samih Baalbaki for his help in checking the Arabic translation of the Interview Schedule; and Mrs Leila Abiad whose typing excellence transformed my handwriting into a legible manuscript.

Finally, words simply cannot express my deep feelings of gratitude to my wife Doris and daughters Rima and Nadia. They shared with me the trials and tribulations of the return to student life.

London *Farid A. Muna*
November 1979

1 Introduction

This book is about the Arab business executive, his managerial thinking and behaviour and how these relate to his wider environment.

The Arab executive's managerial behaviour is heavily influenced by society's social structure and by the values, norms and expectations of its people. For instance, the executive's role within his community and organization is shaped to a considerable extent by the expectations of relatives, friends and employees. The top executive, by virtue of his position in the organization, sees himself as the head of a family: employees are perceived as members of that family. Society's influence is similarly reflected in the executive's distinctively Arab styles in decision making, management of conflict, and interpersonal relations.

In turn Arab executives also influence their society – they are not merely passive. There is a dynamic interrelationship between the executives and their Arab environment. The executives are continually introducing and fostering changes within their organization, community, and society. And their influence extends not only to economic and technological changes but also to changes in social values and norms. For example, Arab executives are deeply concerned with the low value and respect that people in their business community place on time. They are cognizant of the need to instil an industrial work ethic among employees and to develop their organizational discipline.

The executives recognize, however, that deep-rooted values and norms are slow to change. Their efforts at changing the environment are further hampered by the ambivalent feelings they have towards certain social changes which usually accompany modernization. They find themselves in the uneasy situation of introducing into their environment modern and scientific methods and adapting them to their new, yet traditional, work and life styles. In short, Arab executives are agents of social change in a society which itself is undergoing modernization while attempting to retain its Arab identity and character.

Indeed, the Arab executives are taking a leading part in

shaping a critical period in their history. Here is how the Arabs' history and their future potential were described by an Arab-American historian, the late Professor Philip K. Hitti. He ended the 1970 edition of his *History of the Arabs* with these words:

> Originators of the third monotheistic religion, beneficiaries of the other two, co-sharers with the West of the Greco-Roman cultural tradition, holders aloft of the torch of enlightenment throughout medieval times, generous contributors to European renaissance, the Arab-speaking peoples have taken their place among the awakened, forward marching independent nations of the modern world. *With their rich heritage and unmatched natural resources of oil, they should be able to make a significant contribution to the material and spiritual progress of mankind.* (p. 757, emphasis added)

During the 1970s the Arabs began to discover the power of their newly acquired wealth. This power together with the October 1973 war gave them a growing sense of self-confidence and achievement. Thus, if the 1970s can be characterized as their *years of awareness*, then the 1980s are likely to be their *decade of action*. A decade in which the Arabs confront the formidable task of selecting and acting upon courses of action which may contribute to their material and spiritual progress, and possibly that of mankind. The role of the Arab executive in this process is crucial; for he is in a position to influence the selection and to lead the action.

The approach used in this study is to view the Arab executive as an integral part of a business-orientated social system (his organization) which itself is inextricable from the larger social system, its social structure, and in a specific period of its history. Various contributions of social psychology, cultural anthropology, and political science have been woven into the main arguments. To that extent this study is interdisciplinary in nature.

The approach is also eclectic and empirical. It is eclectic in the sense that no attempt is made to develop and test a comprehensive conceptual framework or model, but rather to utilize various perspectives which facilitate the practical investigation of selected managerial issues. It is also based on empirical investigation of executives' attitudes and practices. The bulk of the data were collected from interviews with top Arab executives. Also a small number of expatriate managers with work experience in the Arab world were interviewed in the pilot study. The available literature on the Arab world was helpful, but very little of any substance has been published with direct reference to the Arab business executive. Finally, the author drew upon his own work experience and observations in several parts of the Arab world.

Semi-structured interviews were conducted with fifty-two top Arab executives from six countries: Egypt, Jordan, Kuwait, Lebanon, Saudi Arabia, and the United Arab Emirates (UAE).[1] The executives were either owners or top managers of business organizations ranging in size from 180 to 25,000 employees with an average size of 2480 employees. The organizations they managed were either family-owned, owned by two or more partners, or government-owned. A detailed statistical profile of the executives including their social, educational, and organizational backgrounds is presented in Appendix 1.[2]

The Arab world and its business executives do not exist in an economic or social vacuum. Interaction with non-Arab nations and individuals is inevitable and indeed indispensable. Hence, the importance to non-Arabs of understanding the Arab executive and vice versa. The issues we explore are, therefore, of concern not only to Arab executives and their Arab employees, but also to non-Arab businessmen and expatriates, to consulting and management development organizations, and to social scientists interested in international business and comparative (cross-cultural) management.

The main concern in the present work is to explore selected managerial issues. The study is clearly non-exhaustive in its coverage of topics relating to the Arab executive; also this study does not attempt to compare the Arab executive with his counterpart in non-Arab societies. Comparison is restricted to Arab countries, and references to other societies are occasionally made only to illuminate the topics under discussion. Thus the reader is left to compare the Arabs with whichever society he or she is most familiar. This study is exploratory and the single focus limits the complexity of cross-cultural comparisons.[3]

Using the analogy of a zoom lens, we varied our perspective and range of vision by first focusing on the panorama of the Arab executive's wider environment. We begin by examining the great and continuing influence which the social structure, together with the political and economic developments, have on the mind of the executives. Then we slowly 'zoom in' on the executive's role within his own community and organization.

Without losing sight of the larger social context, we shift our focus to the executive's thinking and behaviour at the individual level. We investigate the Arab executive's decision-making styles, and the extent to which he shares his decision-making power with his subordinates. Social values and norms have significant influence not only on his decision making but also on the power tactics he uses in the management of conflict.

The Arab executive's interpersonal style is characterized by a strong preference for personal and informal (rather than impersonal and formal) approaches of conducting business. This interpersonal style is used by the executive in his relationships with employees as well as with people outside his organization.

From here we move on to the executive's time orientation, and we shed doubt on the widespread view of Muslim/Arab fatalism. The Arab executive's attitudes towards the current modernization process are examined, together with the ambivalence that modernization creates in the mind of the executive. By shifting from one level of analysis to another, our aim is to sketch a portrait of the Arab executive against the background of his changing environment.

The conclusions that can be drawn from this book are set out in the final chapter. Also analysed are the implications of the findings for the training and development of Arab executives; the implications for expatriate employees and foreign businessmen; and the implications for future research.

The research methodology and statistical analyses are relegated to an appendix, as also is the full English version of the Interview Schedule. This leaves the main text less cluttered so that it may be more conveniently read.

NOTES

1. Interviews were conducted in Arabic and English. In this book only the English version of the Interview schedule appears; see Appendix 2. The Arabic translation can be found in F. A. Muna (1979), 'The Arab Executive Mind', Ph.D. thesis, University of London.
2. Appendix 1 also includes notes on the research methodology.
3. It is hoped that the inevitable cultural bias is minimized by the fact that the present author is bi-cultural (Arab and Anglo–Saxon), having studied and worked in the USA and the UK for seventeen years.

2 The Arab Executive and his Environment

> What are the social sciences all about? They ought to be about man and society and sometimes they are. They are attempts to help us understand biography and history, and the connexions of the two in a variety of social structures.
> C. Wright Mills (1916–62)
> *The Sociological Imagination*, p. 40

Who is an Arab executive? First, the executive is a national of one of the Arab countries which together make up the Arab world. Nationals of these countries have a common bond: a strong feeling of identity and commonality. They share the same language, religion, and history. While there are elements of diversity in these three bases of identity, the feelings of brotherhood and common destiny among nationals of Arab countries make it possible in the final analysis to refer to them as Arabs.

Second, Arab executives share the same profession: management of business organizations. Being at the top of business firms, either as owners or managers, they have been conditioned or socialized by common managerial practices and problems. Arab executives are aware of, and influenced by, a commercial and industrial tradition that dates back many centuries, and they share with each other exposure to modern business conditions through formal education and/or interaction with other Arab and Western businessmen. A Jordanian executive from Amman, for example, is likely to have more in common with a Kuwaiti or a Lebanese executive than with a Jordanian farmer.

Third, the societal and business environment in which the Arab executive lives and works has considerable impact on his attitudes and behaviour. The social structure of the Arab world has certain distinctive characteristics which dominate managerial thinking and behaviour. Furthermore, the executives are influenced by the recent political and economic developments in the Arab world, which in turn have a great effect on local and regional business conditions.

ON BEING AN ARAB

The Arab executive is first and foremost an Arab. He is a citizen of one of the twenty-two member countries of the Arab League. These countries, stretching from the Atlantic ocean in the west to the Tigris–Euphrates valley and the Arabian Gulf in the east, have a population of around 160 million people.[1] Arab executives share with each other three closely interrelated bases of identity and commonality: *language, religion,* and *history.*

The *Arabic language* has been singled out by many scholars to be the pre-eminent element in the definition of an Arab. In fact, some go as far as to define the Arabs solely on the basis of the Arabic language.[2] The significance to the Arab executive of this semitic language should not be understated; for in addition to being a key factor of Arab identity, it is the official state language and the medium of expression in daily and business life. Governmental, commercial and labour laws are issued in Arabic; and governments are increasingly insistent on the use of Arabic as the medium of negotiations, correspondence and contracts whereas a few years ago English or French would have been acceptable.

Most Arabs are well aware that for centuries Arabic was a leading language of learning, science, trade, and progressive thought.[3] They are also aware of its limitations, for colloquial Arabic, like most other languages, has suffered from a proliferation of dialects not only between different countries of the Arab world, but even between the various towns and cities of the same country. Nevertheless, classical Arabic remains the common medium of writing, publishing, and broadcasting throughout the Arab world. Finally, Arabic is the language of the Holy Quran, and it is the only language authorized for the performance of the liturgy.

Islam is a second basis for the feelings of identity and commonality. Even if the Arab executive is not a Muslim, he is living in an Islamic environment which has been influenced by Islamic traditions for 1400 years. Moreover, Islam is not simply a religion, it is a way of life.[4] Islamic teachings and laws cover the relations of man to God, men's relations with each other, as well as man's relations towards himself. The duties of man towards the community and those of the community towards man are described and prescribed by Islamic teachings. Although Islam is the stated religion in nearly all the constitutions of Arab countries, the degree of application of Islamic Sacred Law (*Sharī'a*) varies among these countries.[5] Some, for example, Saudi Arabia, still adhere strictly to the Sacred Law in many spheres of life, while others (Egypt for instance) have turned to secular laws for the administration of their economic and social affairs.

The *history* of the Arabs is another source of pride as well as inspiration for the Arab executive, as for many Arabs. If asked to define what they mean by 'the Arab world', most Arabs would include their history as a basis of this common bond. The deep impact this history has on the Arabs was well described by Albert Hourani (1962), when he wrote:

> A full definition (of what is meant by Arab nations) would include also a reference to a historic process: to a certain episode in history in which the Arabs played a leading part, which was important not only for them but for the whole world, and in virtue of which indeed they could claim to have been *something* in human history. (p. 2; Hourani's emphasis)

It was in the seventh century under the leadership of the Prophet Muhammad and his immediate successors that a unified and growing Islamic community was established.[6] The three centuries to follow were to see the Arabs reach their Golden Age under the Umayyad and the Abbasid caliphates. The slow disintegration of the Abbasid empire ended with the fall of its capital Baghdad in 1258. It was the Ottoman Turks who, in the early part of the sixteenth century, consolidated their gains over the smaller dynasties that were the remnants of the old Arab empire. The Ottomans ruled a unified Islamic empire for over 300 years.[7] Their decline was as slow as that of the earlier Arab empires and in the nineteenth century the North African provinces, including Egypt, were the first to be lost to the Ottomans. The First World War put an end to the Turkish rule; but the aftermath of the war saw the Arabs still divided and ruled this time mainly by France and Britain.[8]

During the past thirty years the Arabs have gained their independence. Today in the Arab world, the aspirations, hopes, and dreams of unity persist; but the nearest to any sort of real or permanent unity has been the creation, and most important, the survival, of the Arab League (League of Arab States). Its political achievements, however incomplete and modest, have at least served on occasions to dampen inter-Arab strife. It has also contributed to Arab cooperation in economic, technological, and cultural fields.[9]

THE ARAB AS A BUSINESSMAN

Today's Arab executive has inherited a commercial and industrial tradition that dates back many centuries. This is the case whether the Arab executive comes from the eastern part of the Arab world, the Arabian peninsula, or from the western part, North Africa. For at different periods in their history the Arabs have been, in varying intensity, involved in commerce and industry.

Ancient Arabia lay across the path of the Greek and Roman empires as they spread towards India and China. The Arabs 'were the middlemen of the southern seas, as their kinsmen, the Phoenicians, had been earlier of the Mediterranean'.[10] Commerce and industry flourished under Islam. The founder of the Islamic empire, the Prophet Muhammad, was himself a merchant for a number of years; he grew up in Mecca which was an important centre of trade.[11] The Holy Quran is rich with praise, as well as codes of conduct, for business and trade.[12]

The Arabs' leadership in industry and commerce reached its peak during the Abassid empire (AD 750–1258). The 'extensive international trade' attained was supported by 'extensive home industry and agriculture'.[13] Textiles, glass, furniture, metal, paper, and food products were the main commodities manufactured and exported. According to historians, the economic decline of the Arabs accelerated rapidly with the discovery of the Cape of Good Hope in 1498.[14] That event 'diverted the course of international trade from the Arab East and substituted the Portuguese for the Arabians and Syrians as the middlemen. The Arab lands were thus commercially bypassed'.[15] Together with the discovery of America in 1492, the Mediterranean lost its position as the 'highway of international trade'. That sea, writes the historian Hitti, had 'to wait three and a half more centuries before it could regain its position ... thanks to the opening of the Suez Canal in 1869' (Hitti, 1970, p. 728). Meanwhile, the Arabs lay dormant while the Industrial Revolution was taking place in Europe. With the West's discovery of Arab oil however and its re-discovery of the strategic position of the Arab world, there began a modern industrial and commercial era.

The old mercantile mentality which had flourished for so long still survives, but is now blended with the new industrial mentality.

THE ARAB AS AN EXECUTIVE

Today, the Arab executive directs and is responsible for the operations of a business organization engaged in one or a combination of economic activities such as manufacturing, trade, or service industries. The typical executive manages a business firm, often one that has been his family's for many years; or he heads an organization that he has recently created; or he directs an organization which was either established by government or is now government-owned.

A new type of organization which is slowly gaining prominence in the Arab world is the stock company. Some of these firms were established under joint-venture arrangements either by Arab governments or private businessmen. An example of a new joint-stock company is the Sharjah Group Company formed in 1976. This company describes itself as 'the first Arab Gulf company to have offered its shares exclusively to Arab nationals. As a result of this policy the company is now owned by some 35,000 Arab shareholders and gives us a truly Pan-Arab identity'.[16]

Only a few of these Arab companies are at present open to the public, and their shares sold on stock exchange markets in cities such as Beirut, Kuwait, or Amman. The stock exchanges are relatively new creations. The largest is now the Kuwait Stock Exchange which was formally established in the mid-1970s. Yet, despite its youth, the Kuwait Exchange (trading restricted to Kuwaitis) had in 1978 an overwhelming turnover of $5 billion in only thirty-six stocks – around 13 per cent of the total turnover in ordinary shares at the London Stock Exchange for the same period.[17]

In countries declaring themselves as socialist (such as Algeria, Egypt, Iraq and Syria), the strategic industries and services (usually large organizations) are now state-controlled. For example, the Egyptian Government owns the country's iron and steel company (24,000 employees), and the vehicle assembly company (11,000 employees).[18] Chief executives of national organizations in these countries report to the ministries of industry, finance, or trade. With very few exceptions, all other Arab governments own and run their airlines, railroads, public utilities, and their essential natural resources industries such as petroleum.

The educational background of Arab executives also varies. Some attended only high school, others graduated from universities either in the Arab world or overseas. In the Arab world, modern university education has been available since the nineteenth century. One of the oldest universities, the American University of Beirut, was founded in 1866 by American missionaries, when Lebanon was still under Ottoman rule. And while under French and British occupation, the universities of Algiers, Cairo and Damascus were established in 1879, 1908, and 1923 respectively.[19] At present, nearly all Arab countries have founded their own universities.

Executives who were educated overseas attended universities in the United States and Europe (usually Britain or France). In the present study, 50 per cent of the executives interviewed received their university degrees from the West, 35 per cent obtained their degrees from universities in the Arab world, and 15 per cent attended high school but did not obtain a university degree. The combination of education (whether at home or abroad) and the exposure to the West (through business or personal travel) has typically resulted in a bilingual Arab executive. All the executives in this study, for instance, spoke at least one foreign language, usually English or French.

SOCIAL STRUCTURE: A MOSAIC[20]

The Arab executive lives and works in a society whose social structure, with all its contrasts and diversity, has some distinctive features which have considerable impact on him. It is a social structure in which three different types of social communities co-exist and interact (tribal, rural, and urban). It is a social structure in which social and economic differentiation has begun but many remain incomplete; a social structure in which family and friendship still dominate many spheres of life.

In the Arab world today, political leaders, kings and rulers were born and brought up in three types of social communities: tribal, rural and urban.[21] Although all now reside and work in their respective capital cities, one finds, for example, that most of the state rulers in the Arabian peninsula have their roots in a tribal society; while some political leaders take pride in their village upbringing; and others were raised in cities in their respective countries. Similarly, business executives may have spent their formative years in these different communities. In our present study, for instance, 6 per cent of the fifty-two executives had a tribal background, 48 per cent came from villages, and 46 per cent from cities.

Despite the strong interdependence between these three types of communities, each has remained distinct in its demographic characteristics and economic life style. Much has been written on the stereotypes of the bedouin as a pastoral nomad; the villager as a poor peasant; and the city dweller as a worker, merchant, or administrator. These stereotypes could, however, give the misleading impression that the bedouin, villager and city dweller 'are completely different kinds of people'.[22] For while there are sharp contrasts in their life styles, there are also several socio-cultural traits and customs which they have in common.[23] For example, all three types of communities have a strong kinship structure as a basis for their social organization. Thus the clan remains the basis of tribal society, while the extended family in rural and urban communities plays the important role that the clan does in the tribe.[24] Members of all three types of communities also value loyalty to the clan or family; they value pride, manliness, and hospitality.

These are some of the values and norms to which the Arab executive and his employees were exposed during their formative years whether they were brought up in a tribal, rural, or urban milieu. The influence of these socio-cultural characteristics on managerial behaviour and the expectations they create in the minds of executives and their employees, will be discussed in greater detail as they become more relevant to the findings of this study.

At this point a closer look at the social structure of the executive's environment will be useful. By social structure we mean the patterns of relationships between members of society as these relationships manifest themselves in institutions, groups and roles.[25] The Arab executive lives in a society where family and friendship remain important and prevalent factors even in the functioning of formal institutions and groups. Consequently, we shall find that the Arab executive relies upon family and friendship ties for getting things done within his organization and society.

Societies differ in their degree of differentiation among economic, political, educational, religious, and kinship institutions. In primitive societies, on the one hand, these institutions and the functions they perform overlap considerably, that is they are largely undifferentiated. On the other hand, institutions in highly industrialized societies are highly differentiated, separated and specialized. The Arab society, not unlike many third-world societies, is only partially differentiated.[26] These societies were described by Riggs (1964, p. 38) as 'prismatic' in which the differentiation process has started but may remain incomplete indefinitely.

It is generally accepted that the importance of family/kinship ties is inversely related to the functional differentiation of society.[27] This variability and diversity could range from the undifferentiated tribe, where kinship looms large, to the highly industrialized countries where the nuclear family is the order of the day, and where this nuclear family is 'the anchoring point for most members of society'.[28]

If we view the social structure from the viewpoint of group patterns, we still find that the most distinctive feature of Arab society is the pervasiveness and importance of kinship ties in group affiliation and group interaction.[29]

As in all societies, small groups in Arab society are formed on the basis of *primordial ties* such as family, school or neighbourhood friendship, regional and religious affiliation – as well as other *competing ties* and loyalties such as political party, trade union, or profession. However, the strength of such ties, and the types of them that are important, differ from person to person, from time to time, and from society to society. In Arab society, it will be argued that it is the former *primordial ties* which are generally the more pervasive and more important. Moreover, it will be hypothesized that, as a result, the Arab executive relies heavily on highly personalized and highly informalized methods and styles in the management of his organization.[30]

It is upon these small groups that the larger organizational, professional, and governmental institutions are superimposed. Most frequently, however, the larger groups and institutions exist as 'organizational shells' or 'extraneous façades'[31] within which the smaller groups, factions, and cliques carry out their important activities.

The importance of these small groups is further augmented when their role in relation to the class structure is examined. In their excellent analysis of Middle Eastern social structure, here is how Bill and Leiden (1974) describe the effects of these groups on class structure:

> The overall social structure might best be viewed as a divided grid or creased mosiac in which the intricate web of groups is *partially* partitioned by class lines. Both group and class structures relate to one another reciprocally, and it is this reciprocity that builds coherence into the sociopolitical system. . . . *Group fissures within classes are numerous and deep enough to weaken class cohesion and to retard class consciousness. Loyalty to primordial groups such as family takes precedence over loyalty to class'.* (p. 89, emphasis added)

It is this mosaic of a social structure which constitutes the background for this study of the Arab executive. A social structure in which three communities (tribal, rural, and urban) co-exist and interact sharing several socio-cultural values and norms. In turn, these values and norms influence the behaviour and expectations of executives as well as their employees. It is also a social structure in which family and friendship ties dominate the partially differentiated formal institutions and groups.

RECENT POLITICAL AND ECONOMIC DEVELOPMENTS

Five closely interrelated developments have shaped and continue to shape current political and economic conditions in the Arab world: the increasing emphasis on nationalism and tradition; the creation of the state of Israel in Palestine; the discovery and exploitation of petroleum; the unprecedented economic boom in the region; and the establishment of Arab trade unions.

The low degrees of political stability and predictability within the Arab world have been major factors in conditioning the Arab executive's attitudes towards profit, risk, long-term investment and planning. In addition, the discovery of petroleum and the economic boom of the 1970s, while creating unprecedented business opportunities for the Arab executive, have been accompanied by severe and often peculiar business and social problems.

Emphasis on Nationalism and Tradition

Political instability in the Arab world is a result of several factors two of which are relevant to our present purposes: inter-Arab friction and the Arab–Israeli conflict. The strife between Arab countries stems to a large extent from the varieties of political and economic ideologies adopted by the various countries. In principle, every Arab country considers itself an integral part of the Arab world, and most of them state this goal in their constitutions. However, the Arabs differ on the means of achieving Arab unity and/or the political and economic systems best suited for the prospective united Arab states.

Arab nationalism, as an ideological movement, was at first concerned with issues of independence from the Ottoman Turks and later from European rule. Soon after independence the emphasis shifted to the idea of an Arab nation, and Arab unity became its goal. However, Arab countries differed sharply on economic, political and social issues. For example, some countries, such as Egypt, Syria, Iraq, and Algeria adopted a form of 'Arab socialism'.[32] Their economic and political conditions called for 'radical' changes to enhance economic and political development. Others, such as Saudi Arabia, Kuwait, Jordan, and Tunisia chose to retain their political systems and their 'free enterprise' or in some cases 'mixed' economic systems.

These ideological differences only added fuel to the existing regional and individual rivalries among Arab countries. Furthermore, the abortive attempts at political unity seemed to increase the friction between them. These inter-Arab conflicts have been affecting business conditions and activities as manifested by the occasional border closures, restrictions of trade and the absence of an effective common market. In fact, 25 per cent of the executives interviewed stated that inter-Arab conflicts, and the resultant lack of coordination and cooperation between Arab governments, represented a major problem which they face when conducting business within the Arab world.

Of special interest in this connection is the increasing prominence currently being given in various parts of the Arab world to Islamic principles and ideology. The emergence of oil as a rich and strategic commodity has brought into play local, regional, and international factors that favour adherence to the established teachings of Islam. An increasing number of Arab leaders now feel that there is no need for the Arabs to choose between 'alien' ideologies, such as capitalism and socialism, conservatism and liberalism, democracy and authoritarianism. Instead, they feel that these choices are unnecessary if only the tenets of the Islamic *Sharī'a* are applied as the guiding principles of economic, governmental, and community life.

The desire to maintain both the Arabic and Islamic identity has gained prominence not only in political circles, but also among Arab academics and businessmen. This view, for example, was expressed by several executives during the interviews when asked if they would like to 'voice an opinion' on topics related to business in the Arab world.

Since relatively little is widely known about this view, a few statements by its leading exponents will be helpful. Sheikh Ahmed Zaki Yamani, the Minister of Petroleum and Mineral Resources in Saudi Arabia, argues that the Islamic *Sharī'a* is fully implemented in his country, and is capable of meeting contemporary issues and solving them:

> ... one ought to look at the *Sharī'a* metaphorically as an organic creature, growing, developing, and evolving; attached with a strong link of interdependence to its society, adapting to its needs, and changing with different circumstances. The *Sharī'a* must be viewed as an adequate system meeting the needs of society at any particular interval in history. However, its intrinsic value is not in this momentary adequacy, but in its capability to satisfy the requirements of an ever changing society.[33]

Sheikh Yamani goes on to conclude that Islamic countries which rely on the *Sharī'a* principles can indeed avoid the necessity of making a choice between the economic or political systems of East or West.[34] More recently, the Saudi Minister of Interior, Prince Nai'f Ibn Abdul Aziz Ibn Saud (a son of the founder of the Kingdom), stated that:

> The Islamic *Sharī'a* is the all-inclusive framework of life in the Kingdom of Saudi Arabia. It is not merely the source of law that governs criminal matters but it is also the source of all laws, regulations, orders, decrees and rules that govern all aspects of private and public life.[35]

Other top government officials from the Gulf States have expressed similar beliefs about the role Islam could play in the political, economic, and social developments of their countries. Mr Abd al-Rahman Al-Atiqi, the Kuwaiti Minister of Finance, stressed the need to re-examine certain economic precepts imported wholesale from the West in the light of the *Sharī'a* provisions:

> I would like to point to a system which we have perhaps unnecessarily ignored while being dazzled by the West's achievements, our Islamic economic system ... Islam is not a faith that stands in the way of economic growth. We do not need to abandon our values and traditions at every obstacle we meet. Instead we are called upon to transform it into a creative power and a source of strength.[36]

Indeed, it was the late King Faisal of Saudi Arabia who set the tone for many of the rich countries in the Gulf area when he declared in 1974 that he wanted his country 'to achieve rapid economic growth and modernization without sacrificing the traditions of Islam and Arab culture'.[37]

The Creation of the State of Israel

The creation of Israel had a significant impact on the economic, political, and social aspects of life in the Middle East. While a detailed analysis of this politically loaded subject would be beyond the scope of this study, a few points will be enumerated

THE ARAB EXECUTIVE AND HIS ENVIRONMENT   17

which are particularly relevant to the Arab executive, his actions and his orientations.

1. In the past thirty years four wars were fought (1947–8, 1956, 1967, and 1973), with hundreds of skirmishes and counter-retaliations. A vast amount of wealth has been spent on men and weapons, with detrimental effects on the economies of all the warring factions. The Arab–Israeli conflict continues to be a major factor of political and economic instability in the region, especially for countries sharing borders with Israel.
2. The presence of a large Palestinian refugee population (presently about 2.5 million) has contributed directly or indirectly to several crises in the Middle East (for example Jordan in 1970 and Lebanon from 1975 to date). It is now universally recognized that the Palestinian question is the heart and crux of the Arab–Israeli conflict. The presence of such a large number of stateless refugees in several Arab countries (including the Gulf States) continues to be a potentially explosive problem for the region, with possible world-wide repercussions.
3. The creation of the state of Israel and its aftermath have added considerably to any remnants of anti-Western attitudes the Arabs may have had from past colonization. The West's support of Israel continues to alienate a large number of educated people including Arab executives who, otherwise, would prefer the West over the East if such a choice were necessary.
4. One outcome of the creation of the Israeli state was the pressure it occasionally brought to bear on the Arab states to consolidate their efforts in order to face a common foe. Most recently, however, it has created serious inter-Arab conflict and disagreement over the bases and means which should be considered for reaching a just, comprehensive, and peaceful solution to the Palestinian problem. This inter-Arab conflict tends to disrupt business plans and hinder Arab economic cooperation.
5. Finally, the Arab–Israeli conflict has prompted the Arab countries to use economic sanctions in an attempt to bring about a solution. Initially, the economic boycott was utilized. Business firms trading with and/or supporting Israel are still being boycotted – with varying degrees of success. More

recently, the Arabs have used their enormous oil and monetary resources to apply pressure on some of the major world powers in order to reach an 'equitable' solution to the Palestinian problem. While gaining improved recognition of the existence of the problem, it is not yet clear how successful this pressure will be.

The Discovery and Exploitation of Petroleum

The discovery of oil may well prove to be a major turning point in the history of the Arabs. Although oil was discovered and exploited as early as the 1920s in Iraq, and during the 1930s and 1940s in the Arabian peninsula, the greatest impact on the economic, political, and social spheres of the oil-producing countries began in the 1960s. Through nationalization of the oil companies in some countries, joint-ownership plans (participation agreements) in others, and finally through the medium of the Organization of Petroleum Exporting Countries (OPEC), the oil-rich countries are now able to reap the benefits of ownership and/or control of their oil resources.[38] Needless to say, this development continues to have wide-ranging effects on the economies both of producing and consuming countries.[39]

In the Arab world itself, the oil wealth not only transformed the oil-producing countries, but had substantial influence on the non-oil-producing countries. First, the increasing demand for manpower was met, in part, by the non-oil Arab countries. Second, the rising consumer and governmental demands for food products, manufactured goods, and services were, again, partly met by the non-oil countries. Third, the oil producers have provided their Arab neighbours with large amounts of financial aid and long-term loans, thereby stimulating their economic development and reducing their earlier dependence on non-Arab foreign aid. Fourth, because of this oil wealth and the power it commands, there occurred a shift in the political power-centres in the Arab world. The countries of the Arabian peninsula, especially Saudi Arabia, have become major economic and political powers in the Arab world. Lastly, the oil wealth has fuelled an unprecedented economic boom in the whole region. Because of its significance to Arab executives, let us take a closer look at this boom and its consequences for business conditions.

THE ARAB EXECUTIVE AND HIS ENVIRONMENT 19

Economic boom
The unprecedented economic boom in the oil-producing countries has encouraged the establishment of welfare states able and willing to provide generous employee and public benefits. The long-term economic development and modernization plans of these countries call for massive government investments designed to provide free education, free medical care, modern forms of communication and transport; and finally, the establishment of a viable economic base on which to build manufacturing, banking, and shipping industries that are not totally dependent on petroleum resources.

These development plans are often carried out within the framework of a three-, four-, or five-year government plan. Other large-scale projects are being financed through regional cooperation. Some of the inter-Arab projects, for example, have been promoted by the Organization of Arab Petroleum Exporting Countries (OAPEC).[40] Four well-capitalized companies have been formed by OAPEC since early 1973. The Arab Maritime Petroleum Transport Company has undertaken maritime transport of oil and all related products. The Arab Shipbuilding and Repair Yard Company (established 1974) runs the largest, newly constructed, dry dock in the Gulf area designed to service tankers and ships. The Arab Petroleum Investments Corporation invests in oil refineries, petrochemical complexes, and other related industries. Finally, the newly established Arab Petroleum Services Company provides Arab states with oil exploration and other services previously handled by foreign enterprises.

Many other joint ventures have been formed in the fields of banking, investment and finance, and consumer industries. Some of these projects were undertaken in partnership with the governments and/or large corporations of the major industrialized countries.[41]

Developmental plans, however, are currently hampered in many cases by shortages of manpower, materials, and equipment. Furthermore, the necessary economic infrastructure is frequently found wanting. The manpower shortage, especially skilled and managerial, is acute. This is true not only for government agencies but also for industrial and commercial organizations. Thus, for instance, when the fifty-two Arab executives were asked to mention the problems which they presently faced, 69 per cent considered the manpower shortage to be a major problem. If we exclude the nine Egyptian executives, none of whom faced this problem, then the percentage of executives jumps to an overwhelming 84 per cent.

In those countries with a manpower shortage there is a great dependence on expatriate manpower. This condition has prevailed since the discovery of oil – despite the continuous efforts of the governments and the oil companies to recruit and train local manpower.[42] If we consider the labour law of Saudi Arabia as representative of other laws in the Gulf states, we will have a notion of the general manpower situation. The Saudi Arab Labour Regulations (Article 45) provides that the number of Saudi employees shall not be less than 75 per cent of the total number of the employer's work force. However, this ratio has been reduced by the Minister of Labour when the required technical skills or qualifications are not available in the country. The provision, therefore, is evidently intended as a goal and it has not been strictly applied during the current economic boom.[43]

Manpower shortages in other industries (that is, non-oil) seem to be as severe. Unfortunately, reliable data are not available for comparative purposes. However, even a casual observer visiting the Gulf area would readily notice the relatively large number of Indian, Pakistani, Malaysian, and recently South Korean and Filipino employees working there. Future needs and demands for expatriate manpower are likely to increase as both governmental and private enterprises expand their operations. Meanwhile, the sources of manpower from some of the non-oil Arab countries are drying up, as evidenced by the tougher restrictions these countries are imposing on their own work force in an attempt to control the manpower drain.[44]

For the Arab executive who finds himself faced with the need to recruit expatriate staff, there are at least two problems. First, he must enter what has been aptly described as a 'recruitment jungle'.[45] The competition for skilled and managerial manpower is severe and difficult; and when the desperately needed employees are recruited, the executive becomes concerned with the problem of *retaining* these employees. One Kuwaiti executive, commenting on this problem, stated that for many expatriates 'Kuwait is a mere transit lounge'. The second problem concerns the difficulties of understanding and motivating a multinational

THE ARAB EXECUTIVE AND HIS ENVIRONMENT   21

staff. In some companies in the Gulf area the number of different nationalities working together ranges between thirty and forty.[46] The manpower shortage in the Gulf area has created a 'multicultural and multinational' Arab executive.

The presence of large numbers of expatriate employees with different attitudes, behaviour, and life-styles has thus been influencing Arab executives and employees in profound ways. This phenomenon was dramatically described by a visiting American behavioural scientist as the often ignored side of the 'double-edged culture shock'.[47] This exposure to the expatriates and some of its consequences (both functional and dysfunctional) to the Arab executive is examined in more detail in Chapter 7.

The pace and the strength of the economic boom in the Arab world (especially in the oil-producing countries) accentuated several existing problems which in turn continue to have serious consequences for the Arab executive. For example, the economic infrastructure in nearly all the Arab countries constitutes a major obstacle to business efficiency. The inadequate systems and facilities for communication, transportation, public utilities, and housing were seen by 31 per cent of the executives interviewed as major obstacles. The results of intensive efforts by both the public and private sectors to alleviate these obstacles are slowly being seen. And it seems likely that the pressure will be reduced within the next 3–5 years.[48]

Another problem mentioned by 27 per cent of the executives was the inability of governmental agencies to cope with the rapidly changing economies of the region. For example, the commercial and business laws legislated were either an emulation of foreign laws enacted without careful consideration to the needs of the local environment; or were laws passed expediently to solve a short-term crisis without regard to their long-term effects, and thus partially reflecting lack of proper local or regional long-term planning. Some executives felt that many of the laws passed were not fully understood by the governmental agencies entrusted to execute them. Other executives added that these laws were frequently cancelled or reversed – thus adding considerably to the uncertainty and riskiness of conducting business.

Another closely related problem, seen by Arab executives as a major constraint on business performance, is the apparently massive inefficiency of government agencies in processing routine activities. Of the Arab executives interviewed 64 per cent mentioned the problem of government 'bureaucracy and red tape'. To combat this problem the Arab executive uses his family or friendship contacts (connections) in order to get the work done faster. This, of course, taxes his time and energy, as we shall see in Chapter 6.

Finally, the economic boom has naturally created enormous business opportunities for the nationals of the oil-producing countries. Thus, the national while employed in the larger firms usually at the middle or lower organizational levels, finds himself faced with the challenge and opportunity to participate in lucrative 'on-the-side' business ventures. The manpower shortage, the governmental restrictions discouraging non-citizens from owning small business firms, and the increased demand for goods and services, all combine to induce the national employee to act as the commercial agent, the local representative, or a provider of the 'legal umbrella' for a foreign firm. Or he may find himself engaged as a partner in a local firm, owner of a small service establishment, or active in real-estate sales and development. Clearly, these practices may have detrimental effects on organizational morale and productivity, thus increasing the burdens of middle and top management.

The Arab Trade Union Movement

With a few exceptions, no serious independent labour union movement has developed in the Arab world. In those countries where workers are permitted to organize, their unions are either deliberately created by the ruling single-party system, or they are closely controlled by the governments in power.[49] Either way, the economic and political role of labour unions has been confined to supporting the existing political system.[50]

Nevertheless, labour unions have contributed to the betterment of workers in two ways: direct and indirect. Their direct contribution was in the formation of the International Confederation of Arab Trade Unions (ICATU) in 1956; and the creation in 1965 of the Arab Labour Organization (ALO) – an agency of the Arab League fashioned after the tripartite system of the International Labour Organization (ILO). These two organizations have been instrumental in (a) prompting various Arab countries to enact new and progressive labour laws; (b) establishing centres for education and technical training; and (c) maintaining close relations of cooperation and consultation with the ILO.

Indirectly, labour unions – or rather the fear of labour unions – motivated those countries prohibiting such unions to pass highly developed labour laws, often with the cooperation and help of the ALO and ILO. In addition, the oil wealth enabled the governments of the oil-producing countries to implement generous social security (or insurance) laws, progressive retirement plans, employee home-ownership schemes and various other employee benefit programmes. These have reduced the economic incentive for workers to organize.

In summary then, recent political and economic developments have a great and continuing influence on the mind of the Arab executive. The internal ideological conflicts, coupled with the external political events, are bound to increase the unpredictability and instability of the region, and hence the uncertainty of business conditions. The executive's time horizons and attitudes toward risk, profit, and other business-related activities will reflect these uncertainties. Additionally, the pace of the economic boom and the problems stemming from the inadequate economic and organizational infrastructures are burdening the Arab executive with social as well as business problems which are peculiar to that region of the world.

NOTES

1. United Nations, *Demographic Yearbook* (1978).
2. See Nuseibeh (1956), *The Ideas of Arab Nationalism*; Berger (1962), *The Arab World Today*; and Jabra (1971), 'Arab Language and Culture'.
3. Hitti (1970), *History of the Arabs*, p. 4.
4. Hitti (1971a), *Islam: A Way of Life*; van Nieuwenhuijze (1971), *Sociology of the Middle East*, among many others.
5. The sources of Islamic Sacred Law (*Sharī'a*) are the Holy Quran; the *Sunna* (the practices and traditions of Prophet Muhammad); *Ijmā'* (the consensus of Muslim jurists); and *Qiyās* (analogical deductions).
6. For a short history of the Arabs, see Hitti (1971b), *The Arabs: A Short History*; and Nutting (1964), *The Arabs*. For a long and detailed history, see Hitti (1970), *History of the Arabs*.
7. With the exception of Morocco.
8. Italy occupied Libya for about thirty years; Spain occupied southern Morocco and the Sahara for about forty years.
9. MacDonald (1965), *The League of Arab States*, pp. 284-6.
10. Hitti (1970), p. 44.

11. Lewis (1970), *The Arabs in History*, pp. 34-5.
12. Rodinson (1974), *Islam and Capitalism*, pp. 12-19 and *passim*.
13. Hitti (1970), pp. 343-9.
14. Lewis (1970), pp. 157-8; see also Hitti (1970), pp. 728-9.
15. Hitti (1970), p. 728.
16. Sharjah Group Company *Annual Report*, 1977. For a recent article on this company, see *International Management*, vol. 33, No. 9 (September 1978), pp. 62-4. Several companies were formed by OAPEC (Organization of Arab Petroleum Exporting Countries) in the mid-1970s; they are discussed in the last section of this chapter.
17. *The Financial Times* (London: 26 February 1979), p. 18. Turnover in ordinary shares in 1978 totalled £19.2 billion (around $39 billion); source: *Financial Statistics*, Central Statistical Office (London: HMSO, March 1979) p. 134.
18. For articles on these two companies see *International Management*, vol. 33, Nos. 7 and 9 (July and September 1978).
19. This excludes Islamic universities, some of which are many centuries old. The oldest, Al-Azhar University in Cairo, was established in AD 970. It now has a faculty of commerce. For details on dates and number of students, see *The World of Learning, 1978-79*, vols. 1 and 2 (London: Europa Publications, 1978).
20. The term mosaic was coined by Carleton S. Coon, in reference to the Middle East; see his book *Caravan: The Story of the Middle East* (rev. edn, 1958).
21. This typology is used by many scholars from various disciplines; see Berger (1962); van Nieuwenhuijze (1971); and Gulick (1976), *The Middle East: An Anthropological Perspective*.
22. Gulick (1976), pp. 54-61.
23. *Ibid.*, p. 61.
24. Tomeh (1970), 'Reference-group Supports Among Middle Eastern College Students', pp. 156-65; Prothro and Diab (1974), *Changing Family Patterns in the Arab East*, pp. 70-3; and Gulick (1976), pp. 42-6.
25. The concept of social structure is used widely in social sciences and with a variety of meanings. The above definition draws on works by Radcliffe-Brown, (1940), 'On Social Structure', pp. 1-12; Blau, (1976), 'Parameters of Social Structure', pp. 315-35; and Stinchcombe (1965), 'Social Structure and Organizations', pp. 142-93.
26. Riggs (1964), *Administration in Developing Countries*; Eisenstadt (1964), 'Social Change, Differentiation, and Evolution'; and Farsoun (1970), 'Family Structure and Society in Modern Lebanon'.
27. Moore (1969), 'Social Structure and Behaviour', p. 306; see also Goldthorpe (1975), *The Sociology of the Third World*, pp. 128-44.
28. Moore (1969), p. 306.
29. Eisenstadt (1964); Farsoun (1970); Melikian and Diab (1974), 'Stability and Change in Group Affiliations of University Students in the Arab Middle East'; and Gulick (1976).
30. See Chapter 6 for development of these points.
31. Bill and Leiden (1974), *The Middle East, Politics and Power*, pp. 60-1.
32. Sharabi (1966), *Nationalism and Revolution in The Arab World*.

33. Yamani (1972) 'Islamic Law and Contemporary Issues', p. 53.
34. *Ibid.*, p. 81.
35. *Al-Bilād* (Riyadh), 15 October, 1976, p. 5. From an address by H.H. Prince Nai'f to a regional conference on the application of the principle of *Sharī'a*, 9-13 October, 1976, Riyadh.
36. *Middle East Economic Survey* 'Atiqi on Investment in Arab World', 7 November, 1977, pp. i-vi.
37. MEIRC, S.A. (1977) 'A Summary Analysis of the Labour Movement in the Middle East and North Africa', January 1977, p. 4. This issue will be examined in more detail when we discuss social change and modernization in Chapter 7.
38. Sampson (1975), *The Seven Sisters*. OPEC membership in 1979 included seven Arab countries: Algeria, Iraq, Kuwait, Libya, Qatar, Saudi Arabia, and United Arab Emirates; and six non-Arab countries: Ecuador, Gabon, Indonesia, Iran, Nigeria, and Venezuela.
39. For a discussion on the economics of Arab oil, see Casadio (1976), *The Economic Challenge of the Arabs*.
40. OAPEC was established in 1968 and now includes: Algeria, Bahrain, Egypt, Iraq, Kuwait, Libya, Qatar, Saudi Arabia, Syria, and United Arab Emirates.
41. Casadio (1976), pp. 119-25.
42. For an excellent analysis of the origins of the manpower shortage, see Badre and Siksek (1960), *Manpower and Oil in Arab Countries*.
43. MEIRC, S.A. (1976c), 'Labour and Social Insurance Regulations: Saudi Arabia'.
44. A private discussion with the Jordanian Minister of Labour, Amman, Jordan, June 1977. In addition, Lebanon and Egypt have passed similar restrictions aimed at the regulations of employment policies covering their nationals working in neighbouring countries.
45. MEIRC, S.A. (1978), 'A Summary Analysis of the Labour Movement in the Middle East and North Africa', p. 12.
46. *Ibid.*, p. 12.
47. A private discussion with Dr H. C. Hayward, March 1976.
48. *The Financial Times*, 'Arab Transport' (London: 18 December, 1978).
49. In the Gulf area, the labour laws of Saudi Arabia, Qatar, United Arab Emirates, and Oman do not permit the formation of labour unions. In Bahrain, the law permits the formation of unions but, so far, none has been formed.
50. Hazen and Mughisuddin (1975), *Middle Eastern Subcultures*, pp. 143-8.

3 Social Pressures and the Executive Role

> All the world's a stage,
> And all the men and women merely players;
> They have their exits and entrances;
> And one man in his time plays many parts.
> W. Shakespeare (1564–1616)
> *As You Like It*, II, vii, 139

Social pressures impinge on the Arab executive's attitudes and behaviour. These pressures impose on his time, energy, and performance. In the first part of this chapter we examine the nature and extent of these pressures. In the second part we 'zoom in' and focus more closely on the Arab executive at the micro-level by examining his role in his community as well as in his organization.

SOCIAL PRESSURES

The Arab executive is viewed as a person who is at the helm of an organization which, in turn, is perceived as a business-oriented social system embedded in the larger systems of community and society. Viewed from this perspective, we may regard the executive as both a *target* and an *agent* of social influence and change.

One helpful way of conceptualizing the executive's environment is depicted in Figure 3.1. The political and economic sectors of the environment were briefly examined in the preceding chapter, and the major business-related problems were also highlighted. In this section our focus is on the social pressures stemming from the wider systems of community and society. Of course, one must bear in mind that the conceptual separation shown in Figure 3.1 is only meant to simplify social reality and aid in its analysis.

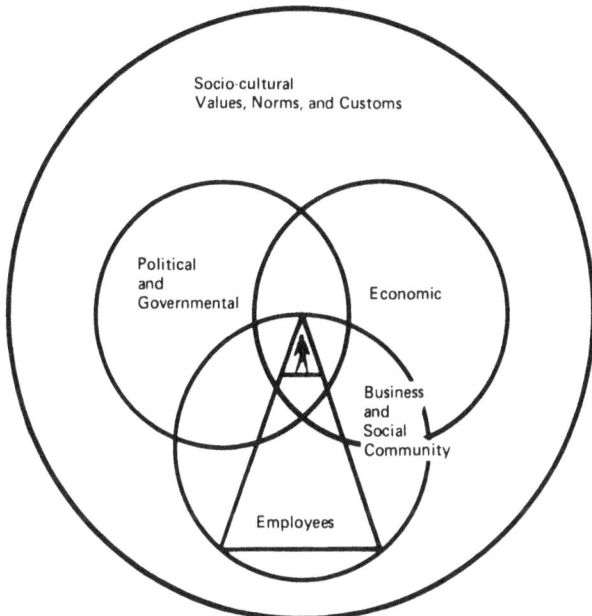

FIG. 3.1 The executive and his environment

The term social pressure refers here to the expectations, demands, or constraints which society places on its members. These pressures can be seen as the price of membership which individuals must pay to belong to a social system. In turn, these expectations, demands, and constraints originate from, and are shaped by, the socio-cultural values, norms, and customs. As in all societies, these values, norms, and customs (often summed up by the term culture) have their roots in a long history of traditions, in religion, and past and present philosophical, political, or economic ideologies.

A large number of social pressures were mentioned by the fifty-two Arab executives. However, only those mentioned by three or more executives are summarized in Table 3.1. Although closely interrelated, these pressures are categorized into those that stem from the wider society (socio-cultural) and those pressures from the executives' immediate business and social communities. We discuss very briefly each of these pressures, leaving until later an explanation of how they influence the executives' managerial and interpersonal styles.

TABLE 3.1 Social pressures as reported by Arab executives (N=52)

Socio-cultural		Business and social community	
Type	Frequency of mention*	Type	Frequency of mention*
1. Low value of time	19	1. Fusion of business, social, and personal life	18
2. Lack of industrial mentality	10	2. Reputation in community	17
3. Restrictions on women	9	3. Top-man syndrome	11
4. Individualistic approach to work	6	4. Social visits at the office	10
5. Dislike of manual work	4	5. High expectations for success	5
6. Marketing constraints	3	6. Nepotism	3
7. The week-end problem	3		

* It must be pointed out that the frequency of mention shown in this table is a conservative estimate of social pressures as felt by Arab executives. This is because open-ended questions were utilized and therefore the above responses were *volunteered* by the executives. Now that these pressures have been identified, future research on this subject will do well to use more structured questions.

Socio-cultural Pressures

Low value of time
Nineteen Arab executives voiced concern over the low value which their fellow countrymen place on time. The examples given by the executives range from lack of punctuality in time schedules and appointments; procrastination and 'tomorrow' *(buqra)* attitude; to a general lack of respect for time. Moreover, this seems to apply to many people: from employees and clients, to government officials. Interestingly, these nineteen executives were nationals of all six Arab countries, and were almost equally distributed among these countries. There will be a fuller discussion of this serious problem in Chapter 7 when we examine the executives' own attitudes towards time.

Lack of industrial mentality
Closely related to the above, this attribute was seen by ten executives as a constraint on their performance. This attribute is exemplified by the lack of industrial discipline in such things as aversion to systems and procedures, lack of organization (especially delegation), and a non-professional attitude toward business. Again, the ten executives were nationals of all six Arab countries.

Restrictions on women
Nine executives considered the societal restrictions on women – especially their exclusion from the work arena – as a constraint on their organizational performance. Five out of the nine executives were from Saudi Arabia; two were Lebanese executives who were referring to their extensive business operations in Saudi Arabia; and two were Jordanian executives who had women on their payroll but complained that it was difficult to include them in the social activities of their companies. Although women in the other four Arab countries are, comparatively speaking, far from being liberated, none of the executives from these other countries considered the present level of women's involvement in business as a serious problem.[1]

Individualistic approach to work
Six executives (from five countries) felt that Arab employees are individualistic as exemplified by a preference to work alone

rather than in a team; and by the tendency to take sole credit for good deeds and to pass the blame to others, or to circumstances, when things go wrong.

Dislike of manual work
Three Saudi Arab executives and one UAE executive expressed displeasure regarding the dislike of manual work by the nationals of their respective countries. These executives felt that 'it is a shame that our young men demand only clerical and administrative work'.

Marketing constraints
Three executives felt that societal values and norms restrict certain types of advertising or marketing. For example, one executive in the consumer industry complained that he cannot advertise certain women's garments and articles in many parts of the Arab world. Another executive felt that door-to-door selling and mail advertising may take years before it is acceptable. The third executive pointed out that the Arab consumer (including the industrial buyer) often bases his buying decision on the personality of the salesman rather than the quality of the product being sold, and/or after-sales service offered.

The week-end problem
For those executives whose business is highly interrelated with western companies, there exists the problem of two week-ends in which communications are difficult for $3\frac{1}{4}$ to 4 days out of each week. The week-end for Arab companies is usually Thursday afternoon and Friday, meanwhile the western firms observe Saturday and Sunday as their week-end. Only three Arab executives mentioned this as a practical problem which they face, but if the volume of business with foreign companies increases it is likely that this problem will be felt by more Arab executives, as well as the foreign businessman.

Pressures from the Business and Social Community

Fusion of business, social and personal life
This heading refers to the inability of executives to separate business affairs from social or personal life. As one executive put it: 'In the West one may be able to compartmentalize his

business life, his social life, and his personal life, but it is not easy in the Arab world . . . they are often one and the same.' This was a problem for eighteen Arab executives from all six countries. Both employees and outsiders (clients, suppliers and government officials) would call on them at home and on week-ends to handle business problems. Also, many of their social affairs are meant to enhance the business. These executives felt *compelled* to accept this sort of pressure in order to remain successful.[2] Only a minority of four executives indicated that they have been able to escape this pressure by making it well known to employees and outsiders that evenings and week-ends 'belong to me and my family'. The remainder of the executives did not seem to see this pressure as a problem – for, either they encourage this practice, or they willingly accept it as part of their work even though it taxes their time, energy, and family life.

Reputation in community
The executives were asked to name those people whom they take into consideration when making personal decisions; in short, people whose opinion and approval matter. Twenty-eight executives said that what mattered was the opinion of family members, close friends and/or employees. This was an expected response since the reference groups and 'significant others' to most persons usually are a small circle of family, friends and work groups: those people whom one knows personally and is affiliated with.

What is interesting, however, is that as many as seventeen executives mentioned the 'larger' community as their reference group, or those whose judgement and approval matter. This community includes those people whom one knows personally as well as those people one does not know. Here, these executives repeatedly mentioned the word reputation – often family reputation. They felt that this reputation is at stake if one did not conform to the community's norms and expectations. Indeed, three of these executives said that when travelling (within Europe) they are able to relax and 'let their hair down'. One executive said: 'I don't care what people think or say when I am in London, for example.' In short, these seventeen executives (from five Arab countries) felt that the community is exerting a pressure on them to which they must *conform*. Perhaps some are conforming to the social pressure because they consider it correct and right (that is they have internalized the community's values and norms); others may be conforming because they feel that the cost of membership in the community is not too high. It is not our purpose here to determine the reasons for conformity, but it is interesting, nevertheless, that several executives voluntarily stated that they do lead a different life-style when they are in an alien country.

Of the remaining executives, four said they 'did not care what people would think or say'. Three others preferred not to express their views on that question.

Top-man syndrome
The top-man syndrome refers to the insistence by clients, suppliers, and government officials on dealing only with the head of the organization. Eleven executives (from five countries) considered this an unnecessary burden on their time and energy.

There are two aspects to this problem. First, there is the feeling among outsiders (clients, suppliers, and so on) that only the top man of an organization can get things done: their trust and confidence is often in the person rather than in the organization. As one president of a large company (over 10,000 employees) put it: 'They [clients] insist on my presence during the negotiations.... They are offended if I am not personally involved.... I am unable to delegate these things to my specialized subordinates.' Another executive complained: 'People with a problem come here and demand to see me; they start from the top instead of starting from where the problem eventually gets solved.'

The second aspect concerns the executive's inability to escape from his many ceremonial duties such as invitations to social events, conventions, and various other ceremonies. Although these executives accept their role as formal representatives of their organization,[3] it is the *excessive* pressure on their time which troubled them.

Social visits at the office
Ten Arab executives (from four countries) were annoyed by the custom of close friends who would drop in to the office for non-business chats over coffee or tea. This phenomenon is closely related to some of the items discussed above such as

value of time and the fusion of business, social and personal life. It is difficult for the busy and over-burdened executive to discourage such custom since it stems from the strong societal norm of hospitality.[4] There were a few executives who actively discouraged this custom, but as one executive said: 'It takes time before we can change these deeply-rooted habits.' Another executive from the Gulf area – who incidentally considered himself a maverick not only in breaking this custom but also with his management style – admitted to having two offices in the same city, mostly to escape from such visitations by friends and colleagues. In some respects, those executives who slowly and carefully discourage these customs can be considered as agents of change in their respective countries. More will be said about this role shortly.

High expectations for success
Five executives, three from Kuwait and two from Saudi Arabia, felt that they were under great pressure from friends, colleagues, and government officials who expect them to succeed in any new venture they undertake. One Kuwaiti executive said: 'After receiving our university education we came back with no work experience . . . we had no models to follow . . . we were the pioneers and the older generation could not advise us and yet their expectations were always high.' A Saudi executive stated that government officials often approve industrial projects and the formation of new companies in which he is involved expecting – or rather taking for granted – a successful outcome. This type of pressure was well described by a Lebanese executive who works closely with executives from the Gulf area: 'These men took charge of large companies when they were still young and with little, if any, on-the-job training. . . . The pressure on them is high. . . . it is really unfair to them.'

Nepotism
The struggle against nepotism was reported by only three executives – two Lebanese and one Jordanian. One executive indicated that many of his relatives are 'angry at him', because of the self-imposed regulation prohibiting nepotism in his organization. But he quickly added that his help to his close-knit extended family takes the form of financial assistance and educational grants. The rest of the executives seemed willing to

accept this strong socio-cultural pressure to hire relatives, although four of them considered it a potential burden since they had ultimately to accept the final responsibility if the relatives' performances were poor.

Two main observations are possible when we analyse the social pressures enumerated above. First, there are both similarities and differences among the six Arab countries in terms of the social pressures felt by the executives of these countries. Thus, for instance, executives from all countries complained about the low value of time; lack of industrial mentality and the fusion of business, social and personal life; while, on the other hand, restrictions on women, dislike of manual work, and the high expectations for success were more keenly felt by executives from the Gulf area.

A brief word on women's status in the Arab world. Although restrictions on women differ vastly from one country to another, the trend towards female emancipation has accelerated in most Arab countries, possibly at a relatively faster rate than was the case for Western women some fifty years ago. In Kuwait, for example, one finds women employed in business organizations and government agencies. Indeed, one of the largest Kuwaiti contracting companies is headed by a Kuwaiti woman.[5] We shall examine the executives' attitudes towards women in business later on in Chapter 7.

Second, the Arab executives facing these social pressures can be viewed both as targets and agents of social influence. We have seen that some of them are actively discouraging those socio-cultural values and norms which they regard as an unnecessary burden on their time, energy, and performance. Examples were provided in which a few executives attempted to minimize the following social pressures: fusion of business, social and personal life; social visitations at the office; and nepotism. The majority of executives, however, seemed either willing to accept these pressures as a price of membership in society, or did not consider these pressures as burdensome.

THE EXECUTIVE ROLE

The examination of social pressures in the preceding section leads us to the important question of what specific behaviour is expected by those people around the Arab executive, by virtue of his position in the community and in his organization? In short, what role is the Arab executive expected to play in his immediate community and in his organization? Let us first examine his role in the community.

Role in Community

For the Arab executive, the community consists mainly of his extended family, friends, business associates, and government officials. From each of these groups the executive is aware of a set of expected activities; a role which he feels obligated to carry out. And with each role there is usually a pattern of reciprocal obligations and claims.

The essence of reciprocity is the give-and-take characteristic in which people are often mutually dependent on one another. In this section, we shall emphasize the executive's obligations, the 'giving' aspect, while the 'taking' aspect will be examined in Chapter 6. First, we will consider the executive's role with his extended family.

We pointed out in the preceding chapter the important part that the extended family plays in the rural and urban communities of the Arab world. Recent studies indicate that the extended family has maintained its importance in spite of the economic development and modernization process now taking place in the region.[6] Prothro and Diab (1974) conclude that 'even though the extended family is not living in one household, it is nevertheless a strong social psychological reality'.[7]

In view of these findings, the executives were asked to describe their relations with their extended family. Based on these descriptions, their answers were coded into three categories: extremely strong, strong to moderate, and weak.[8] Not surprising for the Arab world, relations with the extended family were extremely strong for 67 per cent of the executives, 27 per cent described them as strong to moderate, and only 6 per cent said that they were weak. It must be re-emphasized that although the extended family is often physically scattered, family ties and relations are still strong. Thus, a few executives mentioned that although their relatives are living in many parts of the world, yet they maintain strong family ties (correspondence, visitations, financial assistance, and so on). Modern living and working conditions have, as expected, physically separated the extended family; but it seems, at least so far, that the psychological bonds remain strong.

The patriarchal family system is still the basis of Arab society.[9] Research studies on group affiliation of Arab students at the American University of Beirut showed, in 1958, that the family had a clear preference over other loyalties such as the nation, political party, or religion. When the study was repeated in 1971 there was a slight decline in religious affiliations but the family still came first.[10]

It is interesting, for instance, that when Arabs meet their countrymen for the first time, they usually attempt to establish each other's family identity. In the West, on the other hand, it appears that the initial conversation revolves around a person's occupation or profession. In Japan, introductions are made with reference to one's organization or company rather than profession.

The importance of the family becomes more apparent when we investigate the responses of the fifty-two Arab executives to the open-ended question about the expectations of their extended family. Thirty-nine executives (75 per cent) mentioned that their extended family demand and receive from them all sorts of help and assistance. Some of the more frequently mentioned examples include:

(a) consultation on personal problems or family decisions;
(b) employment in his organization or other organizations with which he is associated;
(c) contacts or pressure on government agencies or other institutions (that is to act as the intermediary);
(d) family visitations and/or maintaining family contacts and ties;
(e) financial assistance and loans.

Some executives, when asked to give additional examples, replied: 'All kinds of help is expected . . . all kinds that the mind can imagine.' In fact, four of the thirty-nine executives described their role as the 'leader of the family', or the 'head of the family', and one even described himself as the 'godfather' of his extended family. Needless to say, these demanding roles add to the executive's existing responsibilities and burdens, and are especially taxing on his time.

Of the remaining executives, six viewed their role as limited to maintaining contact through visits, correspondence, and the telephone; or as one executive put it 'a need to maintain roots'. Finally, seven executives felt that there were very little or no expectations from their extended family.

The executive's role toward his friends, business associates, and government officials is also distinguished by the prevalence of reciprocal obligations and claims. Let us briefly examine the nature of these obligations. When asked to enumerate the expectations which the community held towards them and to describe their role in their community, forty-nine executives were able to describe a variety of expectations. Only three executives felt that they had no role to play in the community, and that the community had no expectations of them by virtue of their positions. The replies given by the forty-nine executives were wide-ranging but described quite similar patterns. The most frequently mentioned examples were:

(a) *Social responsibility.* Under this general title the following expectations were mentioned: efficient management of one's organization; development of the industry in which the executive is engaged (innovation and being kept up-to-date); and the recruitment and training of local national employees. The executive is also expected to give opinion and guidance to friends, associates, and government officials. In short, the executive is expected to be an active member and a responsible leader in his community.

(b) *Contribution to the national interest.* This heading refers to the expectations (especially by government officials) of contributions to the national economic plans of the country. Many executives felt a commitment to achieve, in the national interest, such aims as economic progress, modernization and industrialization.

(c) *Financial assistance to community.* Executives were expected to extend financial help to those friends and associates who are in trouble, and also to support financially social activities in the community, including charitable groups.

(d) *Intermediary role.* The intermediary role refers to the executive's use of family and friendship ties (and of course his position) to expedite, advance, or influence the course of events in favour of other relatives and friends. In the Arab world, one speaks of having 'connections' or 'contacts' in order to get things done faster or as desired.[11] Here, the executive is usually at both the giving and receiving ends of this reciprocal activity. (His own extensive use of this method will be examined in Chapter 6.)

(e) *Link between organization and community.* Executives saw themselves as the crucial link between their organization and its community. This role includes public relations activities such as enhancement of company reputation and standing, and official representation of the organization in the community. This role is akin to Mintzberg's (1973, p. 56) 'spokesman', 'liaison', and 'figurehead' roles. Of course, these are the roles which provide unique opportunities to the effective executive who turns these obligations to his advantage.

It is quite likely that most of the above activities are performed by chief executives from all parts of the world. However, the significance lies in the important nuances such activities have in various societies. Note, for example, that for the Arab executive there is the lack of political affiliation or activities; the lack of organized pressure from labour unions or consumer groups; and the heavy emphasis on the executive's intermediary role.

So far we have perhaps overstressed one aspect of the executive's role in his community; namely the concomitant obligations of that role. Let us briefly examine the other side of the coin. The top executive of an organization, while discharging some of the above-mentioned obligations, is in a unique position to act as his organization's *radar* scanning the environment for vital information, pertinent events and trends, business opportunities, and so on. The ability to do this is similar to what has been called the 'helicopter view', or the ability 'to see the forest from the trees'. It was referred to by some as the *conceptual* ability of top management as contrasted with the interpersonal and technical skills of middle and lower managerial levels.[12] Similarly, Katz and Kahn advocate that organizational leaders must adopt the external perspective (or system perspective) in order to avoid stagnation or failure:

> External perspective is in part a *sensitivity* to environmental demands, to the requirements that organizations must meet in

order to maintain a state of equilibrium with its environment. In part external perspective involves a *sensitivity* to environmental opportunities, to the possibilities of achieving a more advantageous relationship with the environment. Finally external perspective requires *sensitivity* to trends and changes in the environment, which is characteristically in a state of movement both with respect to the demands it makes on organizations and the opportunities it affords to them. (Emphasis added.)[13]

This 'sensitivity' to processes in the environment, along with the ability to foresee how the organization fits within that environment, are executive-level skills. These skills can be learned and achieved by the executive if he is willing to cultivate the obligations and the opportunities provided by his role in the community.

Role in Organization

It was mentioned earlier that the family is one of the dominating social institutions in Arab society. We also referred to the strength of the extended family. The question that comes to mind is whether executives and their employees bring with them to the work organization any of these strong values and norms? In order to explore this topic we asked the Arab executives how they viewed their role in the organization? And what they perceived as the main expectations which their employees held towards them? Responding to these open-ended questions, the executives gave the following answers. Twenty-three executives (44 per cent) described themselves as the *chief executive* of their respective organizations. These executives used a variety of terms to describe this chief executive role. Here are some examples: the leader; the 'motor' of the company; the decision maker; the person who is responsible for the profitability and growth of the company; and various other functions and duties relating to the 'good management' of the organization. In most cases these twenty-three executives also mentioned that their employees expect good wages, good working conditions, promotion, training, and help in personal and family matters. For convenience, this role will be referred to as the *chief executive role*.

What is interesting, however, are the responses of the other twenty-nine executives (56 per cent). These executives perceived their organization as a *family*, and they described their roles using familial terms. Thus, of the twenty-nine executives, eleven saw their role as the 'head of a family'; eleven more described their role as a 'father'; six used the term 'elder brother'; and one saw himself as the 'godfather' of his organization. In contrast to the *chief executive role* let us refer to this role as the *family role*.

Immediately, one would suspect that the executives who saw themselves in the family role are in charge of smaller organizations, or they are possibly the heads of family-owned organizations. In short, is the *family role* related to size or type of ownership of the organization? Looking at the findings, as shown in Tables 3.2 (a and b), the answers to these questions are unmistakably in the negative.

TABLE 3.2(a) Executive role and organizational size*

	Family	Chief executive	Total
Small (180–499)	10	8	18
Medium (500–999)	7	7	14
Large (over 1000)	12	8	20
Total	29	23	52

$\chi^2 = 0.4$; not significant.
*Size = number of employees.

TABLE 3.2(b) Executive role and organizational ownership

	Family	Chief executive	Total
Family-owned	12	8	20
Partnership	9	11	20
Government-owned	8	4	12
Total	29	23	52

$\chi^2 = 1.68$; not significant

Using the chi-squared (χ^2) test, we can ascertain that there are no statistically significant relationships between executive role and organizational size or type of ownership. Similar tests were used to see whether or not family role is related to the executive's age, or his education. Again, no significant relationships were found. It is interesting to note, however, that the younger executives were more likely to describe their role as the 'elder brother', while the older executives would use the terms 'father' or 'head of family'.

An explanation of the phenomenon of *family role* can be found, in part, when we examine how the Arab executives perceive their employees' expectations. Other than the usual demands for increased wages, better working conditions, promotions, and so on, the executives felt obligated to help employees with their personal and family problems (both financial and emotional). Employees' expectations, as seen by the executives, included 'kind and humane treatment', 'care', 'respect', 'control', and 'guidance'. These were some of the terms used by the executives; the examples of help to employees ranged from assistance with governmental agencies (getting a passport, a visa, or even cancelling a traffic violation); advice about housing problems or a divorce; to providing guidance regarding the children's education or future.

A classical self-fulfilling prophecy seems to be at work here: employees' expectations (and behaviour) towards the executive reinforces his perception of his role as a 'father'. Alternatively, the executive's behaviour towards his employees is paternal and this reinforces the employees' perceived role as members of a family. Either way, it seems that both parties' expectations of one another coincide. Let us briefly look at the employees' attitudes on this matter. Although employees were not included in this study, there are some research findings which supplement and support the present study. Research studies by MEIRC, S.A. were carried out in three oil companies operating in three Gulf countries.[14] The main results of these studies indicate that the Arab employees interviewed ($N=205$) had three expectations of what they considered as a 'good' manager. First, employees expected to be 'treated well' by their manager and their organization. For the employees, a good manager would treat his employees in a considerate and humane manner. He would be interested and willing to provide good services and facilities as well as 'care and guidance' to their personal problems, on and off the job. This is closely related to the expectations as seen by the executive, which is to play the father role. Second, employees expected to be 'paid well' in terms of higher salary levels and improved employee benefits. Third, the employees expected their skills to be 'used well' in their present jobs, and they expected to be trained (in and out of the company) in new skills in order to enhance their future careers.

Unfortunately, the MEIRC studies are the only ones available which shed some light on the expectations of Arab employees. Although these studies covered employees in a specific industry (oil) and region (Gulf area), their findings are relevant and lend support to our investigation of the Arab executive's role in his organization.

In this chapter we began by examining the nature of the social pressures as felt by Arab executives. We discovered that these pressures act as constraints on the executives' behaviour, attitudes, and time. However, we found that these pressures vary from one country to another, and that the reaction of the executives to the social pressures also varied. Thus, while most of the executives accepted many of the socio-cultural values, norms, and customs (thus, being targets of social influence); a small number of executives were attempting to change those values, norms, and customs which they considered as burdensome (thus, acting as agents of social change).

In the second part of the chapter, we investigated the roles of the Arab executive in his community and in his organization. We drew attention to the strength and importance of the executive's relations with his extended family. An attempt was made to differentiate between the obligations and opportunities afforded to the executive, especially by his role in the community. Finally, when examining the executive's role within his organization, it was found that the majority of Arab executives viewed their organization as a family unit. They described their role in familial terms such as father or elder brother. It seems that the executives' expectations coincide with those of the employees in the form of a self-fulfilling prophecy.

NOTES

1. The Arab executives' attitudes towards working women will be examined in more detail in Chapter 7.
2. This group included both the owner/partner and the non-owner executive.
3. This role of a formal representative is termed by Mintzberg the 'fig-

urehead' role. As he points out, it is very likely that executives utilize this role to maintain strong links (informational and friendship) with other businessmen and government officials; Mintzberg (1973), *The Nature of Managerial Work*, pp. 58–60, 126–7.
4. On hospitality of Middle Eastern people, see Antoun (1965), 'Conservatism and Change in the Village Community', p. 7; Gulick (1976), *The Middle East: An Anthropological Perspective*, p. 46.
5. This executive was the subject of the cover article in a business magazine, *Alam Attijarat*, February 1978, pp. 26–7. For further articles on this executive and on women's status in Kuwait, see *The Times* (London: 12 June, 1978), p. iv.
6. Tomeh (1970), 'Reference-Group Supports Among Middle Eastern College Students', pp. 156–65; Prothro and Diab (1974), *Changing Family Patterns in the Arab East*, pp. 70–3; Farsoun (1970), 'Family Structure and Society in Modern Lebanon', pp. 257–307.
7. Prothro and Diab (1974), p. 70.
8. The three categories were based upon the intensity of contact and commitment to extended family. It includes, for example, visitation to and time spent with relatives; emotional and financial support; and other miscellaneous help and support.
9. It is interesting to note in this respect that the middle name for most Arabs consists of their father's name, see Gulick (1976), pp. 39–42, 215–21.
10 Melikian and Diab, (1959), 'Group Affiliations of University Students in the Arab Middle East', pp. 145–59; Melikian and Diab (1974), 'Stability and Change in Group Affiliations of University Students in the Arab Middle East', pp. 13–21; and Melikian (1977), 'The Modal Personality of Saudi College Students', pp. 166–209.
11. Farsoun (1970), pp. 269–70. Farsoun describes the intermediary role as follows: 'The term *wastah* is colloquial Arabic for an "intermediary" a go-between, or the process of employing an intermediary or go-between, "a process of mediation" in almost any and all types of activity' (p. 269).
12. Mann (1964), 'Toward an Understanding of the Leadership Role in Formal Organizations'.
13. Katz and Kahn (1978), *Social Psychology of Organizations*, p. 504.
14. MEIRC, S.A. (1975), "Job Attitude Survey of Saudi and Kuwaiti Employees'; MEIRC, S.A., (1976a), 'Jcb Attitude Survey of Omani National Staff'; and MEIRC, S.A. (1976b), 'Das Island Attitude and Motivation Survey'.

4 The Arab Approach to Decision Making

> Consult them in affairs of the moment, then,
> when thou hast taken a decision, put thy trust
> in God.
> The Holy Quran, III, 159.

In the preceding chapter we have focused on the Arab executive as a target of social influence and control. We delineated the extent to which social pressures act as constraints on his behaviour, energy and time. Our attention in the present chapter will be on the executive as an organizational leader, viewing him as the prime agent of influence and control within his own organization. The ability as well as the capacity to exert influence and maintain control over the actions of others is one of the more common definitions of the power concept,[1] and it is this definition which is used here. In this chapter, we shall be looking at the Arab executive's use of that power in a very important reality of organizational life: decision making.

DECISION-MAKING STYLES

The literature in the field of decision making is immense. The often-made statement that decision making is *the* organizational activity[2] has motivated researchers from a variety of social science disciplines to its study.

From scholars of organizational behaviour came an abundance of literature on leadership and leadership styles – which often incorporated and/or discussed the decision-making process.[3] One facet of this highly complex phenomenon is the executive's choice about how much and in what ways to involve subordinates in decision making.[4]

In the present study we are interested in the extent to which the Arab executive shares his power of decision making with his subordinates under various situations involving different types

THE ARAB APPROACH TO DECISION MAKING 45

of business decisions. We are also interested to find what effects, if any, would socio-cultural, economic, and political factors have on the decision-making styles of the Arab executive. For instance, would factors such as the following have any influence on how 'autocratic' or 'democratic' the Arab executive is when making decisions: the prevalence of paternalistic and familial social patterns; the absence of Western-styled democratic systems; the recent economic boom; and the manpower shortage.

In short, our aims here are (a) to draw a profile of the decision-making styles of executives from the six Arab countries; (b) to analyse the similarities among, and the differences between, these executives; (c) to isolate those variables which provide the best explanation of the variation in decision-making styles; and (d) to provide support for the recent empirical research which emphasizes that decision-making styles are dependent on the interaction between social-structural, situational, and personal variables (often termed situational or contingency approach).[5]

The conceptual framework and the methods used in this study of decision-making styles reflect borrowing from several research studies dating back forty years. Table 4.1 summarizes the relationships between this author's approach and those used in prior investigations. As can be clearly seen, the latest two studies (Heller, 1971; Vroom and Yetton, 1973) had a substantial influence on the present approach.

Decision-making style is defined and measured by a four-point equal interval scale reflecting the various degrees of power sharing between the executive and his subordinate(s).[6] The power-sharing continuum is illustrated in Figure 4.1. An almost similar continuum was used by Heller (1971) which he called the influence-power-sharing continuum (IPC). The only difference between the two continua is that ours does not include Heller's style 2 (own decision *with* explanation – see Table 4.1). It was felt that Heller's style 2 cannot be considered a distinct style, but rather an elaboration on his style 1 (own decision *without* explanation); to explain or to 'sell' the decision to subordinates is not likely to change either the power wielded by the executive or the influence exerted by his subordinates on the outcome of a decision he had already made. In other respects, however, we share Heller's inclusion of delegation as an extension to the conventional decision-making styles. It highlights an

TABLE 4.1 Comparison between decisional styles employed in this study and those of previous investigators. (Adapted with modification from Vroom and Yetton, 1973.)

Lewin, Lippitt and White (1939)	Maier (1955)	Tannenbaum and Schmidt (1958)			Likert (1967)		Heiler (1971)		Vroom and Yetton (1973)		Muna (present study)
Autocratic leadership	Autocratic management	Manager makes decision and announces it	Manager sells decision	Manager presents ideas and invites questions	Exploitive authori-tative (System 1)	Benevolent authori-tative (System 2)	Own decision without detailed explana-tion (Style 1)	Own decision with detailed explana-tion (Style 2)	Manager makes decision himself (A1)	Manager makes decision, obtaining necessary information from subordinate (A11)	Executive makes decisions without consulting sub-ordinate(s), but may consult superiors, partners or outsiders (Style 1)
	Consultative management	Manager presents tenta-tive decisions, subject to changes		Manager presents problems, gets suggestions, makes decision	Consultative (System 3)		Prior consultation with subordinate(s) (Style 3)		Manager shares problem with subordinate, makes own decision (C1)	Manager shares problem with group, makes own decision (C11)	Prior consultation with subordinate(s) (Style 2)
Democratic leadership	Group discussion	Manager defines limits, asks group to make decision		Manager permits group to make decisions within prescribed limits	Participative group (System 4)		Joint decision-making with subordinate(s) (Style 4)		Manager and subordinate together arrive at mutually agree-able decision (G1)	Manager (acting like a chairman) and group dis-cuss, evaluate, and make a group decision (G11)	Joint decision-making with subordinate(s) (Style 3)
Laissez-faire leadership							Delegation of decisions to subordinate(s) (Style 5)		Delegation of decisions to subordinate (D1)		Delegation of decisions to subordinate(s) (Style 4)

important, even crucial, managerial responsibility with potentially great benefits to the organization, the manager, and the subordinate. For delegation can serve not only as a motivator to employees (satisfying ego and self-actualization needs), but could also be an excellent managerial training technique. Furthermore, the ability to delegate is an indispensable tool to the executive which, if used properly, could possibly lead to a better management of his own time – especially so for the Arab executive, as will be pointed out throughout this study.

Again, we share Heller's aversion to the use of the term participation in studies on decision making. Indeed, participation is a value-laden concept, reflecting a normative standpoint often with a positive value attributed to it. The term also lacks precision and thus would be difficult to measure. Finally, if the term participation has emotional implications in the West, it is even more so in the Arab world where participation sometimes has the wider connotation of joint-ownership (often government ownership), especially in the oil industry.

A DECISION-MAKING PROFILE

Let us now turn to the results obtained from interviews with the fifty-two executives from six Arab countries. In the decision-making section of the semi-structured interviews, each executive was presented with a description of four alternative decision styles (see Figure 4.1). Each was then given seven decisions and

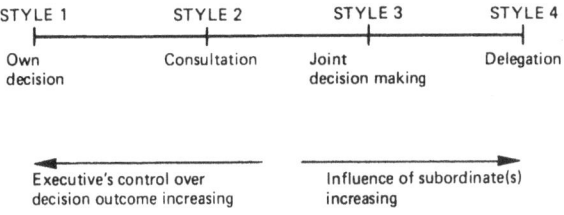

FIG. 4.1 The power-sharing continuum

was asked to describe which of the alternatives he would normally use to arrive at the decision. The author would then code each decision – often after a few minutes of discussion and probing. This procedure minimized response bias. The four alternatives (styles) were:

I. the decision is made for you, no consultation or discussion with subordinate(s);
II. prior consultation with subordinate(s); he/they may or may not influence your final decision;
III. you and your subordinate(s) *together* analyse problems and come to a decision – subordinates have as much influence as you have on the final decision (majority decision);
IV. ask subordinate(s) to make decision on his/their own.

The seven decisions were:

1. The decision to promote one of the employees directly supervised by one of your subordinates;[7]
2. the decision to discipline one of the employees directly supervised by one of your subordinates;
3. the decision to terminate the services of one of the employees directly supervised by one of your subordinates;
4. the decision to reduce the total work force by 20 per cent;
5. the decision to increase the work force in a subordinate's department/division;
6. the decision to introduce a new product, or enter a new market, or take on a new project, or expand existing work facilities (whichever is applicable);
7. the decision to alter/modify the formal organization chart (changes in job and/or responsibilities, re-organization) in your subordinate's department/division.

Two approaches were used to analyse the data; each with its own advantages and disadvantages, as will be seen shortly. The first approach uses the frequency distribution of responses for each of the seven decisions; or it can use the responses of the executives from each of the six countries for all decisions. This approach is meant to emphasize and draw attention to the fact that executives rarely employ only one decision-making style irrespective of the type and nature of the decision. Indeed, executives vary their style in accordance with the problem at hand, as common sense suggests.

Table 4.2 and Figure 4.2 present the results using frequency distribution of reponses by style broken down for each decision and for the total of all decisions. It is clear from Table 4.2 that the four decision styles were utilized on nearly all decisions. There were three exceptions: Style 3 (joint decision making)

THE ARAB APPROACH TO DECISION MAKING 49

TABLE 4.2 Distribution of decision styles for each decision by all Arab executives ($N=52$) (expressed as percentages)

Decision	Style 1 Own decision	Style 2 Consultation	Style 3 Joint decision	Style 4 Delegation	Total
1	8	60	19	13	100
2	10	58	15	17	100
3	10	71	10	9	100
4	51	40	9	—	100
5	8	54	29	9	100
6	52	48	—	—	100
7	19	52	10	19	100
All decisions	22	55	13	10	100

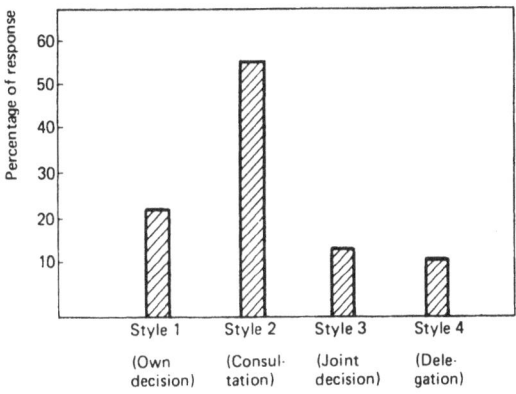

FIG. 4.2 Proportion of responses for all decisions by all Arab executives ($N=52$)

was not employed for decision 6, and Style 4 (delegation) was never utilized for either decision 4 or 6. It is worth noting that both decisions 4 and 6 involved major decisions for the organization.

It is also clear from Table 4.2 and Figure 4.2 that Style 2, consultation, was predominantly preferred by Arab executives for this specific set of decisions. Obviously, a different set of problems is likely to produce a different profile. But consultation, as will be seen later, seems to be the preferred style for Arab executives.

TABLE 4.3 Distribution of decision styles by executives from each of the six Arab countries ($N=52$) (for all decisions) (expressed as percentages)

Country	Style 1 Own decision	Style 2 Consultation	Style 3 Joint decision	Style 4 Delegation	Total
Egypt	35	55	10	—	100
Jordan	32	55	6	7	100
Lebanon	9	66	21	4	100
Kuwait	23	47	8	22	100
Saudi Arabia	17	44	27	12	100
UAE	10	71	2	17	100
All countries	22	55	13	10	100

Using the same approach as above, Table 4.3 shows how the executives from *each* country responded to the seven decisions. This table provides a good description of responses by executives from the various countries. It shows the extent of differences and similarities: it is interesting, for example, to note that none of the Egyptian executives delegated any of the seven decisions. Instead, the Egyptian executives showed a strong preference for only two of the four styles (90 per cent of their responses were for Styles 1 and 2). In comparison, the Saudi Arabian executives varied their choices slightly more evenly among the four styles.

A second approach makes use of the power-sharing continuum and the assumption that its four styles are separated by equal intervals. This assumption allows us to use the mean scores (arithmetic averages) and, more importantly, to analyse the variances among these scores. One potential disadvantage of this approach is that it can give a misleading impression that there is one 'average' decision style. This is not so. As we have cautioned from the beginning of this chapter, managers do employ various styles for different problems and situations.

The following values were assigned to components of the power-sharing continuum (see Figure 4.1): Style 1 (own decision) = 10; Style 2 (consultation) = 20; Style 3 (joint decision making) = 30; and Style 4 (delegation) = 40. Thus, a high score implies that an executive allows his subordinate(s) to share his decision-making power thereby increasing the influence of his subordinate(s) on the outcome of the decision. Conversely, a low score implies a lower degree of power sharing and, consequently, more executive control over the outcome of the decision. Let us first look at the mean scores of executives from *each* country for all seven decisions. The results are presented in Table 4.4. Examining the mean scores in this table tells us that, *in general*, the Egyptian and Jordanian executives interviewed involved their subordinates in decision making to a lesser extent than executives from the other countries. A simple one-way analysis of variance resulted in an F (5,46) equal to 3.48 ($p < 0.01$) indicating that the mean scores of the executives from the six countries are indeed significantly different. This indicates that it will be fruitful to extend the analysis in two ways.

TABLE 4.4 Mean score of executives from each country for all decisions

Country	Mean	N
Egypt	17.6	9
Jordan	18.8	10
Lebanon	21.9	8
Kuwait	23.6	9
Saudi Arabia	23.3	10
UAE	22.5	6
All countries	21.2	52

First, the seven decisions are broken down into three categories. The first category includes decisions 1, 2, and 3, the second includes decisions 4, 5, and 7, and the third includes only decision 6. Statistically,[8] this grouping of decisions showed the highest intercorrelations between the decisions within each category. Conceptually, the breaking down of the seven decisions into three categories follows common sense. Thus, the first category of decisions (1, 2, and 3) relate to personnel problems of subordinates two levels removed from the executive; mainly, the promotion, discipline, and termination of service of an employee who is directly supervised by one of his subordinates. Decisions 4, 5, and 7 contain departmental/divisional problems: substantial reduction of the work force across all departments/divisions; increasing the work force in a subordinate's department/division; and a reorganization of a subordinate's department/division. Finally, decision 6 is an organizational decision with potential serious consequences for the whole organization. It involves a major and a long-term venture requiring large financial outlays or risk taking.

Second, the analysis must be extended to include the other independent variables which may have an influence on the decision process (the dependent variable). Data were collected on a variety of socio-psychological variables such as the size, age, nature, and ownership of the organization; the age, education, social background, status, and country of the executive. The intent here is to ascertain how much of the variance in decision styles can be explained, and to which sociopsychological variable(s) it can be attributed.

TABLE 4.5 Mean score of executives for three categories of decisions

Country	Three personnel decisions (1, 2 and 3) (Mean)	Three departmental decisons (4, 5 and 7) (Mean)	One organizational decision (6) (Mean)	N
Egypt	20.0	15.6	14.4	9
Jordan	19.5	19.2	14.0	10
Lebanon	24.6	20.4	18.8	8
Kuwait	27.8	22.1	12.2	9
Saudi Arabia	25.0	24.4	14.0	10
UAE	23.3	23.1	16.7	6
All countries	23.3	21.1	14.8	52

Let us first examine the responses of the executives from each of the six Arab countries for the three categories of decisions, as shown in Table 4.5. From this table it is clear that the executives interviewed involved their subordinates more in personnel-related decisions than in the organizational decisions. In fact, all the mean scores of executives from each country were consistently decreasing as we moved from personnel to departmental to organizational decisions. This finding corroborates Heller's (1971) conclusions that managers tend to be less autocratic when dealing with problems related to the employees of their subordinates, and more autocratic when facing the more important organizational-level decisions.

This variation in decision-making styles also lends some support to Vroom's general conclusion that 'it makes more sense to talk about participative and autocratic situations than it does to talk about participative and autocratic managers'.[9] Although the situational variables in the Vroom–Yetton model focus on a different set of problem attributes than those used here, nevertheless, the same principle is shared.

Also from Table 4.5, it will be noted that the mean scores of Egyptian and Jordanian executives (on personnel and departmental decisions) are generally lower than the scores of the executives from the other countries. This could be easily misinterpreted if we attribute the lower score solely to the nationality of the executives. To avoid this misinterpretation, we must quickly introduce the effects of the other independent sociopsychological variables listed earlier. These other independent variables may indeed be more closely associated and correlated to decision-making style than the country variable. The questions, therefore, are: which variables are most closely related to the decision-making styles of the fifty-two executives? And to what extent do these variables account for the variance in their decision-making styles?

Since some of the independent variables (country, age, and education of executive, size of company and so on) are interrelated, several spurious relationships may exist which will distort the analysis. However, the multiple regression method helps us to overcome this problem. It controls for any spurious effects and it isolates only those variables which contribute substantially to the variation in decision-making styles. Details of the statistical steps and results are presented in Appendix 1.

VARIABLES AFFECTING DECISION STYLES

It is now possible to discuss the findings for each of the three categories of decisions. Table 4.6 presents a summary of the results. Let us start with the personnel decisions 1, 2, and 3. Multiple regression analyses indicate that three independent variables had significant contributions to the variation in personnel decision-making styles. The three variables are: the age of the executive, his education, and the size of his organization. These three variables taken together account for 22 per cent of the variance in decision style. That is, given these three variables, one can explain 22 per cent of the variation in personnel decision styles.

Taken independently, each of these variables is related to decision styles in some way or another. Thus, the data indicate that the older the Arab executives are, the more autocratic they tend to be – sharing less of their decision-making power with their subordinates. One possible explanation could be that older Arab executives, recognizing that the 'Arab respect for age' syndrome increases their position and referent power, are not as concerned about their subordinates' acceptance of the decision as their younger counterparts. In essence, the older executives can 'afford' to be more autocratic.[10]

The data also show that executives without a university education tend to share more of their power with subordinates when compared to university-educated executives. One can only speculate that those executives without a university education are more likely to rely on experienced specialists, thereby involving these specialists more in the decision-making process. Finally, there seems to be a relationship between the size of the organization and decision styles related to personnel matters. The larger the organization the more likely that its top executive will involve his subordinates with the personnel decisions. This finding was not an unexpected one, as common sense would indicate.

Turning to departmental decisions 4, 5, and 7, Table 4.6 shows that there are two sets of variables explaining the variation in decision styles. One set of variables included only individual attributes, while the other set contained organizational attributes. Therefore, a proportion of the variance in departmental decision styles could be explained using either individual or organizational variables.

The individual variables refer to the executive's occupational status (owner-executive or non-owner executive); his educational background; and his age. These variables taken together accounted for 42 per cent of the variance in departmental decision styles.

Again, if taken independently, each was highly related to decision style. The individual variable accounting for the greatest proportion of the variance is the executive's occupational

TABLE 4.6 Independent variables accounting for the variance in decision-making style. (Three decision categories.)

Personnel decisions 1, 2 and 3		Departmental decisions 4, 5 and 7		Organizational decision 6	
Variable	Direction*	Variable	Direction*	Variable	Direction*
		(A)			
Age of executive	(−)	Non-owner/partner executive	(−)	Lebanon	(+)
No university education	(+)	Arab university education	(−)	No university education	(+)
Size of organization	(+)	Age of executive	(−)		
$R^2 = 22\%$†		$R^2 = 42\%$†		$R^2 = 20\%$†	
		(B)			
		Family-owned organization	(+)		
		Egypt	(−)		
		Saudi Arabia	(+)		
		$R^2 = 43\%$†			

* The (+) or (−) under direction indicates whether the variable is positively or negatively related to the score of decision style.
† R^2 is the square of the multiple correlation coefficient, adjusted for the number of independent variables in the equation and the number of cases. It is a more conservative estimate of variance explained, especially when the sample size is small.

status. Non-owner/partner executives, as might be expected, shared less of their decision-making power with subordinates than executives who owned or partly owned the organization. The non-owner executive probably had to consult or persuade his own superiors (government ministries or a board of directors) before arriving at the final decision, especially since the decisions involved important departmental changes.

Educational background was also found to be related to decision style. The data indicated that the executives who obtained university degrees from an Arab university were likely to be more autocratic than (a) executives without a university degree; or (b) executives who received degrees from Western universities; or (c) executives who received degrees from both Arab and Western universities.[11] It will be interesting to compare the average scores of the executives (for decisions 4, 5, and 7) broken down by level and type of education. It will be recalled, from Table 4.5, that the average score for all executives was 21 for the departmental decisions. The following are the scores moving from the most to the least autocratic: executives with Arab degrees scored 17; those with both Arab and Western degrees scored 20; those with only Western degrees scored 22; and executives without a university degree scored 26.

Lastly, executive age, as in the previous category of decisions, was again negatively related to power sharing; the older executives showed less power sharing than the younger ones.

As mentioned above, the variation in style for departmental decisions 4, 5, and 7 could also be explained by a set of organizational variables (called by some contextual or sociological variables). Three of these variables jointly accounted for 43 per cent of the variance in decision styles. The three variables are: type of organizational ownership; Egypt; and Saudi Arabia. Let us take a closer look at each. Executives from family-owned organizations involved their subordinates in departmental decision making to a greater extent than their counterparts working in government-owned organizations, or in organizations owned by two or more partners.

Executives from Egypt shared less of their decision-making power with their subordinates than executives from the other five countries. Their average score on the power-sharing continuum was significantly lower at 15 when compared to a score of 22 for all the other executives ($p < 0.01$). One probable

THE ARAB APPROACH TO DECISION MAKING 57

explanation is that the business sector in Egypt is highly influenced by the pervasiveness of government rules, regulations, and controls.[12] In fact, during the author's visit to Egypt (while conducting the interviews), the Egyptian Prime Minister in office at that time delivered a speech to several hundred top executives. In his speech the Prime Minister voiced his government's concern about its own restrictive rules and regulations, and he promised the executives that, in line with Egypt's new open-door policy, government restrictions on the internal and external affairs of all companies will be relaxed.[13]

Finally, the executives from Saudi Arabia showed more power sharing in departmental decisions than the executives from the other five countries. A plausible reason might be the heavy reliance by top Saudi executives on highly specialized expatriate and/or other Arab managers. These specialized managers are given more freedom in departmental affairs, thus allowing the Saudi executives to concentrate their time and energy on the more urgent business problems and opportunities so common in a fast-moving economy.

The third and final decision category contains organizational decision 6. Here, as with the previous categories, multiple regression analysis isolated two variables which taken together accounted for 20 per cent of the variance in decision style. The two variables are: Lebanon as compared to the other countries; and executives without university education as compared with executives with a university degree.

The Lebanese executives had an average (mean) of 19 on decision 6 as compared to an average of 14 for all other executives ($p < 0.01$). One can only speculate that, as a result of the 1975–6 Civil War and its aftermath, several of the Lebanese executives interviewed who were doing business outside Lebanon (often from branch offices located outside Lebanon), were more geographically decentralized. Decision 6 is a major organization decision involving large financial outlays and/or high risk; the Lebanese executives interviewed were more likely than not to consult their top subordinates who were in charge of the various geographical centres.

Lastly, executives without university education had significantly higher scores on the power-sharing continuum than their university-educated counterparts. Again, this may reflect their utilization of business specialists – in finance, marketing, or production – whose advice on decision 6 would be essential.

Before proceeding to the next section, it is worth looking again at the frequency distribution of the total responses for the three decision categories discussed above. Table 4.7 summarizes this distribution (this table is a reduction of Table 4.2, shown earlier in this chapter). The table highlights two major results. First, as we move from personnel to departmental to organizational decisions, we notice lesser power-sharing (more autocratic) behaviour from the fifty-two executives. As already indicated, this shows that the importance of the decisions to the organization (a situational variable) is closely related to decision style.[14] The second finding concerns the pervasiveness and dominance of Style 2, consultation, among Arab executives. Consultation has a special meaning for Arabs, and especially so for Arab executives, as we have just seen. Let us take a closer look at this phenomenon.

TABLE 4.7 Distribution of responses by style for three decision categories ($N=52$) (percentages)

Decision category	Style 1 Own decision	Style 2 Consultation	Style 3 Joint decision	Style 4 Delegation
Personnel (Decisions 1, 2, and 3)	9	63	15	13
Departmental (Decisions 4, 5, and 7)	25	49	16	10
Organizational (Decison 6)	52	48	—	—
Weighted average	22	55	13	10

CONSULTATION

There are strong historical roots for consultation in the Arab world, and particularly in the Arabian peninsula where tribal leaders have practised consultation for millennia. It is a norm which is still practised by the present-day rulers of countries in the peninsula. Senior members of the ruling families, or the community, are consulted on matters of importance. The final decision, however, is always made by the leader who may or may not adhere to the advice of his senior men.

Added impetus for the consultation practice was provided by Islam. One finds that consultation is actively encouraged by the Holy Quran and the *Ḥadīth* (the *Ḥadīth* consists of the acts and sayings of Prophet Muhammad and early Islam). Consultation is mentioned several times in the Quran and the *Ḥadīth*. In fact, one of the 114 *Sūras* (chapters) of the Holy Quran is entitled *Shūrā*, that is Consultation. In this *Sūra*, it is revealed that those who conduct their affairs by consultation are among the ones upon whom God's mercy and heavenly rewards will be bestowed (XLII, pp. 36–9).

It is interesting to note that the importance of consultation was emphasized by several executives during the interviews. For example, three executives quoted different verses from the Quran on consultation; significantly, these quotations were volunteered in free response (that is without direct prompting). Similarly, four other executives mentioned consultation when asked which personal traits or characteristics have contributed to their success. Finally, we have seen that 55 per cent of the total responses on decisions 1 to 7 were for Style 2, consultation.

What are the reasons for the prevalence of consultative behaviour among Arab executives? Who is being consulted, and when? Here are some of the reasons and conjectures, made possible through extended discussions with a few of the executives whose time, fortunately for us, permitted such a luxury in what otherwise would be a hectic schedule. Briefly, these are some answers to the above questions:

1. There are strong expectations among senior managers, partners, and even some friends and relatives to be consulted on organizational or daily issues. One executive described it as 'a tradition, a custom... there are always some people whose opinion you must seek, or else they will be hurt and angry'. The same executive reminded the author that this 'custom' applies not only in business organizations, but at the higher levels of family, clan, tribe, or nation.
2. Consultation, for some Arabs, seems to be an effective 'human relations' technique. It is used for several occasions and situations: (a) to avoid potential conflict between an executive and his subordinate; (b) to please, to placate, or to

win over persons who might be potential obstacles to one's ideas or actions; and (c) to provide the person being consulted with a 'face-saving' mechanism which enables him to reply, 'Yes, I was consulted on . . . ', if he was ever asked.
3. There is, of course, the conventional use of consultation during which necessary information is gathered, or genuine guidance and advice is sought.
4. Finally, it must be stressed that only a few 'selected' people are generally consulted. This seems to be the case whether we are referring to a business organization, family, tribe, or nation. Understandably, there is no hard and fast rule for specifying who these selected few are; it is dictated by the situation and the circumstances.

Up to this point we have said relatively little about joint decision making (Style 3). It will be recalled that Style 3 received an average of 13 per cent of the total responses on all seven decisions. An immediate question which comes to mind is why such a low score? One possible reply would be to attribute this low score to the societal context. Thus, in none of the countries included in this study do we find a prevalence of truly democratic practices such as elections, majority rule, and so on. If that is the case, why should one expect a change in the beliefs, attitudes, or behaviour of both executives and their employees once they start working in a business-oriented social system (organization) which is part of the larger societal system? Most persons (including executives and subordinates) would bring to the business organization those same values and attitudes they have been forming ever since childhood.

Another argument of equal relevance would be that Arab executives generally seemed to dislike committee or group meetings. Consequently, on those decisions concerning more than one subordinate, the executives seem to prefer individual-to-individual consultation with each subordinate thereby, *de facto*, avoiding majority decisions. Indeed, Arab executives have a strong preference for personalized and informal methods of conducting interpersonal business affairs – as will be discussed at length in Chapter 6.

Finally, a brief word about delegation (Style 4). This style, receiving the lowest score (10 per cent of total responses), seems to be under-utilized especially if we keep in mind that the fifty-two executives we interviewed were top executives in their respective companies. It is generally believed that the higher in the hierarchy a manager's position is, the more likely he is to delegate non-policy decisions – especially if his organization is large and long-established. Our findings indicate that age of company was not related to style, and that size of company was related to style for only three out of seven decisions.[15]

As mentioned earlier in this chapter, delegation has several benefits to the organization, the top executive, and the subordinate. If delegation is indeed under-utilized, the consequences for the growth and development of the above-mentioned parties could be detrimental indeed.

NOTES

1. Weber (1947), *The Theory of Social and Economic Organization*; Dahl (1957), 'The concept of Power'; French and Raven (1959), 'The Bases of Social Power'; and Cartwright (1965), 'Influence, Leadership, and Control'.
2. Barnard (1938), *The Functions of the Executive*; Simon (1957), *Administrative Behaviour*.
3. For a recent review, see Vroom (1976), 'Leadership', pp. 1527–51.
4. A distinction is made in this study between leadership styles and the styles of decision making. A leader, in whatever type of organization, has a large number of tasks and roles besides that of a decision maker, see Mintzberg (1973). Hence, the term decision-making style is preferred here to the traditionally used term of leadership style.
5. For a leading exponent of the leadership contingency approach see Fiedler (1967), *A Theory of Leadership Effectiveness*.
6. The equal interval assumption is discussed in Appendix 1.
7. Decisions 1, 3, and 5 were adopted, with modifications, from Heller's (1971) questionnaire.
8. Details of the statistical tests and analysis are presented in Appendix 1. Only the final results are reported here with minimal discussion of the statistical methods employed.
9. Vroom (1976), p. 1545.
10. Vroom and Jago showed that managers are more 'participative' on problems requiring subordinate acceptance than on problems that did not, see Vroom and Jago (1974), 'Decision Making as a Social Process', p. 760.
11. Western-founded universities, such as the American University of Beirut (AUB), are referred to in the present study as Arab universities. The curricula are taught in both Arabic and English; and the education took place in an Arab environment.
12. It is widely recognized that the Egyptian bureaucracy and its methods of

managing the public sector have been among the serious obstacles to Egyptian industrial efficiency and progress. See Mabro and Radwan (1976), *The Industrialization of Egypt, 1939-1973*, p. 96.
13. *Al-Ahrām*, 15 January, 1978 (p. 1). In Egypt, all companies are severely restricted in their employment practices. Additionally, government-owned companies are required to obtain government approval even for minor departmental changes.
14. This finding provides further support to the contingency approach recently popular among management and organizational scholars.
15. The average company size in our study was around 2500 employees, while the average company age was 27 years.

5 Conflict Management

> I apply not my sword where my lash suffices,
> nor my lash where my tongue is enough. And
> even if there be one hair binding me to my
> fellowmen, I do not let it break: when they
> pull I loosen, and if they loosen I pull.
> Caliph Muʻāwiyah AD 661–680.

The main interest in this chapter is on conflict between the Arab executive and his immediate subordinate during or after the decision-making process. Specifically, we are interested in the extent of such conflict, and how the Arab executive uses his power to manage it. In general, the Arab executive experiences relatively low opposition from his immediate subordinates. The executive reduces the frequency of conflict either by 'authoritarian' behaviour and/or by frequent consultation with his subordinates. Furthermore, the Arab executive prefers to avoid open confrontation whenever conflict occurs. This is done either through the mediation efforts of a third party or by complete avoidance of the issue in conflict.

There is a wealth of literature on conflict by scholars from a wide variety of disciplines. It covers many types of conflict at many levels, from the international, social, organizational, departmental, to conflict between individuals.[1] There is, however, little available literature on how Arab executives handle conflict in organizational contexts. One would expect that Arab executives would be influenced by societal values and norms in managing conflicts within their organizations. This is what we set out to explore in this chapter.

It is important to note that our concern here is deliberately limited to dyadic conflict along the vertical dimension of a hierarchy (executive and his subordinate) and our interest is on one of the parties to the conflict only – the executive. Lastly, the conflict is over an episode involving a business decision.

Dyadic conflict (conflict between two persons or two social units) is defined as a process in which the actions of one person tend to prevent or force some outcome against the resistance of another person.[2] Thus, an executive may impose a decision against the resistance of his subordinate, or he may intentionally block a decision favoured by the subordinate.

We have already seen in the preceding chapter the extent to which Arab executives retain or share their decision-making power. It was found that, on average, the Arab executive chose to limit his subordinate's influence on decision outcomes. Indeed, the executives chose Style 1 (own decision) and Style 2 (consultation) an overwhelming 77 per cent of the time; both styles tend to limit subordinate's influence. A few questions immediately come to mind: what about opposition or resistance from subordinates, if any, when they do not agree with the decision? How is it handled? And what are the executive's reactions to proposals submitted by his subordinate if he does not favour these proposals?

To answer these questions, the executives were presented with hypothetical incidents in which two types of conflict situations were present. Conflict situation *Type 1* is when the hypothetical issues are favoured by the executive, but opposed by the subordinate. *Type 2* is the reverse: the issues are opposed by the executive, but favoured by the subordinate. Each executive was given two incidents and was asked to describe how he would handle the conflict situations Type 1 and Type 2. One of the incidents involved a personnel-related conflict: a disagreement between the executive and his immediate subordinate about the promotion of a key employee working for the latter; while the other incident was at the organizational level: a disagreement between the executive and his immediate subordinate about an expansion plan (or a new product/project) which involves the department/division of the subordinate. The executives were familiar with the incidents since both were an extension of the decision-making section of the interview to which they had just responded.[3]

Furthermore, each executive was asked to provide a proverb or a saying which guided or influenced his thinking when facing the sort of conflict described above. This approach was designed to add depth to our understanding of the executive's conflict management techniques.

Let us now turn to the results of the interviews. We shall first present a brief summary of the overall findings. Later, we shall discuss the implications of these findings for conflict management. There were five major findings:

1. *Insufficient opposition from subordinates.* Five Arab executives complained that, in general, there was insufficient resistance or opposition from their immediate subordinate(s). They felt that the frequency and magnitude of resistance and opposition were undesirably low. In short, they wished more of their subordinates would act as genuine devil's advocates from time to time. This, of course, would be benefical as long as the devil's advocate role is not institutionalized or systematized, in which case it may become useless.[4]
2. *Open confrontation is taboo.* When irreconcilable positions were reached, neither executive nor subordinate allowed it to develop into direct or open confrontation. Values and norms dictate the use of a third party to convey the message of rejection. The role of a third person (a mediator) in Arab society is crucial in conflict management.[5] Open confrontation is also avoided by the use of other indirect methods to communicate one's position, such as non-verbal behaviour, deliberate procrastination, or even a complete avoidance of the issue.
3. *Consultation reduces conflict.* Seven executives believed that the frequency of conflict was substantially reduced because the immediate subordinate was often consulted, and his opinion taken into account. If the subordinate's advice and opinions are occasionally incorporated into the decision, then to that extent consultation will tend to reduce conflict. If, on the other hand, consultation turns into a ritual where the executive is repeatedly asking for opinions and advice, but then always making decisions contrary to such advice, then conflict might be exacerbated and long-term relationships will suffer.
4. *Reliance on position power.*[6] With the above comments in mind, it was found that for Type 1 situations (executive favours, subordinate opposes) the power tactic most favoured by fifteen executives was 'pulling rank' or going ahead with a decision in spite of subordinate's opposition.

For Type 2 situations (executive opposes, subordinate favours) the power tactic most often used was non-decision making. Twelve executives used such phrases as 'freeze it', 'keep it pending', and 'give it time to die', to describe their non-decision-making tactics.

Finally, many of the executives preferred not to differentiate between Types 1 and 2 conflicts and stated that they would initially attempt to convince the subordinate of their viewpoint by reasoning with him, using knowledge or information only they possess, or will attempt to persuade the subordinate using their 'diplomacy' and 'personal touch'. Failing all that, the executives will resort to their formal authority and power, as described above.

5. *Importance of issues does not change tactics.* The importance of the issues (personnel *vs.* organizational) was related to the likelihood of conflict occurrence. For example, many executives indicated that it is unlikely that conflict will occur over the personnel issue, but may occur over the organizational one.

However, when asked to assume that conflict did happen on the hypothetical personnel issue, an interesting reaction took place. The executives would use the same firm tactics they used for the organizational conflict. This indicates that the importance of the issues at stake is not as relevant as the fact that opposition did occur (albeit, hypothetically). One would expect milder tactics (such as persuasion, bargaining and the like) to be employed; instead, the same tactics as reported above were most commonly used. One is reminded of the several research studies showing that conflicting action (opposition from subordinates) evokes similar reactions (pulling rank or non-decision by executives).[7] Role expectations (such as boss has the final word), clearly influenced the executive's behaviour.

The above five findings, if taken separately, are clear and do not need further elaboration. However, if we examine the first finding (insufficient opposition from subordinates) in relation to the other four, then a contradiction becomes apparent.

One way of explaining the phenomenon would be to take an increasingly popular view which states that, in general, certain kinds of conflicts are not only inevitable but also desirable (functional) to the conflicting parties if effectively managed.[8] This broad statement invites further questions, such as: what level or magnitude of conflict?; how do we effectively manage it?; and so on. These questions are appropriate and necessary, but are beyond the scope of this chapter. However, using this perspective and keeping these questions in mind provides us with a frame of reference, a context, to discuss the findings. Viewed in this context, the five findings can be translated into two observations: (a) the frequency and magnitude of opposition leading to conflict is low – as reported by a number of executives and as observed by the interviewer; (b) Arab executives tend to handle these conflicts in such a manner as to discourage future opposition. What we have here is a classic dilemma – or even ambivalence. A desire for some opposition from subordinates, and a concomitant fear of losing control and influence (power) if the executive yields to the opposition.

Let us look at the first element of this ambivalence: insufficient opposition. The reasons given by some executives for the low occurrence of conflict support the notion that power is often wielded in the following manner:

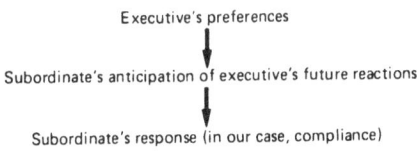

(With feedback loops, of course)

Here is how one executive described it: 'The subordinate gets to know his boss so well he can "read his mind" – he is so eager to please his boss that he is unlikely to think of or engage in activities which may displease the boss. The result ... no opposition.'

This type of executive power is creating subordinate compliance[9] which probably is at an unhealthy level. If a reasonable amount of conflict and opposition does lead to creativity and positive stimulation[10] then subordinate's over-compliance could indeed be unhealthy. (Bearing in mind that we are discussing subordinates at a high managerial level reporting directly to top executives.)

The question, then, becomes: what is a reasonable amount of conflict? Again, it is beyond our present scope: it must be noted, however, that future research on this question must include the norms, expectations, and attitudes towards authority and conflict prevalent in the countries being studied.[11] Nevertheless, the fact remains that a few executives did express their desire for more opposition (devil's advocate role, as some put it).

The other side of the ambivalence equation is the fear of losing power if conflict is encouraged. One Egyptian executive summarized it well: 'If a leader, whether on the national or organizational level, does not suppress opposition, then people (including my employees) would think he is weak, thereby losing respect.'

The solution to this dilemma, *if a solution is desired*, is entirely in the hands of the executive. Two of the several choices he has are: (a) to change the attitudes and predisposition of his employees towards authority, conflict, and power. This is a difficult and a very slow process, but not impossible; and (b) to modify role expectations and/or organizational structure with the aim of creating manageable conflict. This would be done through creation of devil's advocate roles, suggestion box, and other devices to encourage opposition – designed to fit the needs and the climate of the organization at that stage of its growth and development.

The above findings were based on responses from executives who were asked to describe their hypothetical behaviour.[12] However, as mentioned earlier, another approach was used which assessed the executive's values and beliefs about dyadic conflict. This was accomplished by asking each executive to provide a proverb or a saying (in either Arabic or English) which guides or influences his thinking when facing this type of conflict (see Interview Schedule, Appendix 2). The proverbs/sayings told by the executives added further support to the earlier findings.

Twenty-four of the fifty-two executives gave a total of eighteen proverbs/sayings (*all in Arabic*). Here is a translation of three proverbs (proverbs mentioned by more than one executive):

1. Four executives mentioned this proverb: 'Time is a problem-solver', or 'Time solves problems'.
2. Three executives recited this Quranic verse: 'Consult them in affairs of the moment, then, when thou hast taken a decision, put thy trust in God' (III, 159).[13]
3. Two executives referred to the famous words in Arab history attributed to the founder of the Umayyad Caliphate, Muʻāwiyah (AD 661–80). The Caliph Muʻāwiyah, known for his political finesse, was reported to have declared: 'I apply

not my sword where my lash suffices, nor my lash where my tongue is enough. And even if there be one hair binding me to my fellowmen, I do not let it break: when they pull I loosen, and if they loosen I pull'.[14]

The other fifteeen proverbs conveyed various messages most of which can be summarized in a few advisory sentences: be reasonable; avoid extremes; avoid confrontation; be cooperative; and finally, there are many things that an executive ('apex of pyramid') sees, or hears, that cannot and should not be seen, or heard, by the subordinates.

A moment of reflection will show that the values reflected by these proverbs do not contradict the executives' responses as summarized earlier. In fact, they add support to them. Thus, we have the proverb, 'Time is a problem-solver', relating directly to non-decision-making tactics; the Quranic verse associated with the use of consultation to reduce potential conflict; and finally Mu'āwiyah's political finesse of being 'diplomatic but firm', and avoiding head-on confrontation or the risk of 'breaking the hair' which binds the executive to his subordinates.

In this chapter, we have seen that Arab executives, in general, experience relatively low opposition and resistance (low in frequency and magnitude) from their immediate subordinates. This could be partly attributable to their consultative style, as demonstrated in the preceding chapter; but it can also be attributed to the societal values and norms which shun open confrontation and encourage rather authoritarian behaviour on the executive's part. We have also examined the dilemma facing those executives who would like to see increased 'constructive' resistance from their immediate subordinates – bearing in mind that these subordinates are top-level managers. Finally, we were able to look at some of the power tactics, as well as the thoughts behind these tactics, which Arab executives use in managing conflict.

NOTES

1. For reviews and analyses of recent literature on conflict see Thomas (1976), 'Conflict and Conflict Management', pp. 889–935; Nightingale (1976), 'Conflict and Conflict Resolution', pp. 141–64; and Katz and Kahn (1978), *Social Psychology of Organizations*, pp. 612–51.

2. From Katz and Kahn (1978), p. 613.
3. Details of the incidents and the conflict situation are shown in Appendix 2, which contains the complete Interview Schedule.
4. See Thomas and Bennis (Eds.) (1972), *Management of Change and Conflict*, pp. 17-19.
5. Ayoub (1965), 'Conflict Resolution and Social Reorganization in a Lebanese Village', pp. 11-17. Also see Farsoun (1970), 'Family Structure and Society in Modern Lebanon', pp. 257-307.
6. As opposed to other bases of power; reward, coercive, referent, and expert power, to use French and Raven's (1959) typology. A sixth base of power, information power, is usually added by many others.
7. Katz and Kahn (1978); Thomas (1976); Thomas and Walton (1971) 'Conflict-handling Behaviour in Interdepartmental Relations'.
8. Coser (1956), *The Functions of Social Conflict*; Hall (1971), 'Decisions, Decisions, Decisions'; and Katz and Kahn (1978).
9. Even if we wish to use one of Kelman's (1958) other categorizations (compliance, identification, or internalization), the end result for our purposes is the same – minimum opposition from subordinates.
10. Katz and Kahn (1978), p. 641.
11. For example, Melikian found that there is 'a general willingness among Saudi college students to accept the authority of a "boss" and to esteem it ... this acceptance and esteem of authority are accompanied by a willingness to be in that position themselves'. See Melikian (1977), 'The Modal Personality of Saudi College Students', p. 180.
12. Aided by quasi-participant observation by the author during the periods of waiting for and conducting the interviews.
13. Ali, *The Holy Qur'ān: Text, Translation and Commentary* (1975).
14. As quoted in Hitti (1970), *History of the Arabs*, p. 197.

6 Interpersonal Style

> Men's natures are alike; it is their habits that
> carry them far apart.
> Confucius, 551–479 BC

The most distinctive feature of the Arab executive's interpersonal style is his strong preference for a *personal* or person-oriented approach in his managerial activities. In fact, he has a strong aversion to *impersonal* relationships. This, as we shall see shortly, stems largely from the strength of the executive's primordial (family and friendship) ties, as well as from the characteristics of his society's social structure.

This personal approach is a dominant feature in four important behavioural aspects of interpersonal relationships. The four aspects, to be discussed separately in this chapter, are:

1. the use of rituals and customs in conducting business;
2. the use of personal ties and connections;
3. the importance of employee loyalty;
4. the open-door tradition.

A natural consequence of this heavy emphasis on the personal approach is the executive's preference for 'informality' both in the structure of his organization and in his own style of dealing with people. We will be examining this preference for 'informality' in the last section of this chapter.

It must be added at this point that it is these aspects of interpersonal relations which are at once noticed by expatriates and foreign businessmen; and are often the cause of their initial sense of bewilderment or frustration when working with the Arab executive.

RITUALS AND CUSTOMS IN CONDUCTING BUSINESS

When starting a business discussion, the Arab executive will invariably engage in social talk and amenities with his guest for what may seem a long time. The guest is first offered coffee, tea, or soft drinks. Then for a period ranging from 2 to 15 minutes,[1] the executive and his guest would talk about several topics of interest to both parties provided it is *not* the subject of the business at hand. It is generally regarded as 'impolite' or even 'shocking' to start immediately with the business discussion.

Thus, it was not considered unusual to ask the Arab executives whether they engage in this ritual, and how they felt about it. Their responses, as reported in Table 6.1, confirm the prevalence of this ritual. Fifty-one executives (98 per cent) stated that they normally engage in this business practice. Of those, forty-two executives considered it beneficial while the other nine executives felt that it was mostly a waste of time. Only one executive stated that he does not perform or even encourage such practice, viewing it as a total waste of time.

TABLE 6.1   Rituals and customs in conducting business ($N=52$)

Response	Number of executives	With whom?	Why?
Yes, and it is a beneficial custom	42	Employees and outsiders = 10 Outsiders only = 32	Know guest on personal basis Evaluate person and establish trust Cement relations (if guest is known) 'Break the ice' – relax – put at ease
Yes, but it is a waste of time	9	Outsiders only = 9 (mostly with Arabs)	Must do it . . . it is an expected custom Hospitality and tradition
No, it is a waste of time	1	—	Waste of time

What is perhaps more interesting are the reasons given by the forty-two executives who considered this custom beneficial. These reasons include: getting to know the guest on a person-to-person basis; to evaluate the person; to establish trust in the person; to cement relations (if parties already know each other); and finally to 'break the ice' and put the parties involved at ease.

It is also interesting that the nine executives, while considering this ritual as a waste of time, felt obligated to perform it because it was expected, mostly by other Arabs. Tradition and the norms of hospitality prescribed this sort of behaviour. Furthermore, these executives did not employ this practice with their subordinates but only with outsiders such as clients, suppliers, government officials, and other visitors. The nine executives come from all six countries; they had various social and educational backgrounds; were in different brackets; and were from various types of organizations.

The above business ritual seems to be a universal one. Desmond Morris calls it 'grooming talk'. This is how Morris describes the practice during 'formal business encounters':

> Here its expression (grooming talk) is almost entirely confined to the opening and closing moments. *Instead of waning slowly, as at the dinner party, it is suppressed rapidly, after a few polite, initial exchanges.* It reappears again, as before, in the closing moments of the meeting, once the anticipated moment of parting has been signalled in some way. Because of the strong urge to perform grooming talk, business groups are usually forced to heighten the formalization of their meetings in some way, in order to suppress it. (Emphasis added)[2]

However, the duration and purpose of the opening period of social talk differ from society to society. It has been pointed out long ago, by Hall and Whyte, that for Anglo-Saxons, and especially North Americans, the acquaintance and discussion time in business tends to be comparatively short and impersonal.[3] The American businessman, for example, regards acquaintance and discussion periods as opportunities in which he tries to make his point 'quickly, efficiently, and neatly'. Businessmen from many other countries, on the other hand, do not look favourably upon such quick business meetings or what Hall and Whyte call 'the "hit-and-run" school of business behaviour'. Businessmen from various countries not only act differently during the opening period of business discussion, they also do so for varying reasons.

For the Arab executives the use of this business practice can be distinguished in two important ways. First, the reasons given by forty-two executives for engaging in this practice seem to be more *person-oriented* than role- or task-oriented. Executives used such terms as 'person-to-person', 'personalized', and 'personal approach' as contrasted to impersonal, when describing their reasons for engaging in these rituals. Second, these rituals were characterized by their seemingly prolonged duration. This is demonstrated by the responses of the other ten executives who considered the practice a waste if time. It is also demonstrated by the estimated range of 2 to 15 minutes as given by some executives. In brief, the Arab executive tends to dislike *impersonal* and *transient* relationships when conducting business. Here is how one European expatriate working in the Gulf area summarized it: 'You rarely walk into an Arab's office and start by discussing a business problem. After you socialize a bit, you bring out the subject in an "incidentally" or "by the way" manner, even though the problem at hand is an important one ... in the long-run you will be more effective doing it this way.'[4] It seems that the majority of Arab executives would agree with these remarks, especially when *outside* business visitors are involved.

PERSONAL TIES AND CONNECTIONS

The use of personal (family and friendship) ties and connections is not only widespread, but is also an important and necessary means of doing business. This approach is in direct contrast with the reliance upon official, institutional, or formal business channels for conducting business affairs. In the Arab world the use of such personal ties and connections is evident in a wide range of activities. Typical examples that were provided by the executive include; (a) expediting and getting a work-permit, a passport or a visa, and generally bypassing or expediting most governmental formalities and paperwork; (b) obtaining referrals or employment; and (c) knowing about, negotiating, and eventually securing a multi-million dollar business contract.

An explanation for the above phenomenon can be found in our earlier discussions of the social structure and of the executive role (Chapters 2 and 3). In both chapters we examined the nature and the strength of primordial ties based on family and friendship. For the Arab executive, there is a powerful incentive to use personal (family and friendship) ties instead of institutional or formal channels in getting things done. This is partly due to the inefficiency, and sometimes the absence, on institutional systems and procedures; and partly due to the importance of family and friendship ties which are usually more powerful than institutional rules and procedures. This combination of institutional inefficiency and the strength of family and friendship ties leaves the executive without a viable alternative. Time and effort will be minimized if the executive uses his personal ties and connections in lieu of the formal channels. Of course, this sort of activity will, as in a vicious spiral, only increase the inefficiency of the formal systems – at least for those who have weaker ties or connections.

Furthermore, as we have seen in Chapter 3, the executive is under strong social pressures and expectations to play the intermediary role.[5] By virtue of his high position in the community and in the organization, he is expected to wield his power to influence the course of events in favour of relatives and friends. The intermediary role is, however, characterized by its reciprocal nature. In Chapter 3 we emphasized the 'giving' aspect of this reciprocity; we shall now turn to the 'taking' aspect and examine the Arab executive's attitudes on this subject.

The fifty-two executives were asked the following question: 'In your community, to what extent do people rely on family ties, friendships or other means of influence to get things done, or done faster?' All the executives, except one who preferred not to answer, indicated that this practice occurs to a great extent. Their replies varied from 'considerable', and 'very great', up to 'an enormous extent'; with some saying that it is 'the rule rather than the exception' or it is the 'custom'. It is very likely that some of these executives were unconsciously using their experiences in or with the major industrialized countries as a criterion for judgement, while others were explicitly comparing their circumstances with these countries. Not that industrialized countries are immune from this business practice, but the incidence and preponderance of such practices are probably lower.

When asked whether this business practice is a help or a hindrance to them in performing their duties, thirty-three (65 per cent) of the executives indicated that it is a help. Twelve (23 per cent) of the executives felt that it is both a help and a hindrance, and the remaining six (12 per cent) executives considered it a hindrance to their performance. A typical example of how this practice was seen as helpful, is when personal ties are used to 'save time and trouble' in dealing with the formalities of other organizations (especially government agencies). Several of these executives in describing this practice commented that it is a 'necessary evil', saying that it is 'sad' and 'unfortunate' but one must 'play by the rules of the game'. For those executives who considered the use of personal ties as both a help and a hindrance, this practice is a 'double-edged weapon'. Along with the benefits there are usually concomitant obligations; we have already seen in Chapter 3 that the executive's time and energy is taxed partly because of these obligations. Additionally, an executive may be 'influenced' to hire or promote an incompetent employee, thus adding to the burdens of that executive.

Finally, there were six executives who considered this practice a hindrance; they felt that it is an unfortunate form of 'favouritism' in which 'who you know' counts more than 'what you know'. This of course can be detrimental to executives who do not have powerful connections as well as to those who do. As one executive pointed out: 'Because of my organization's dependence on my personal connections, efficiency and performance often suffer whenever I am on a holiday, an extended business trip, or for any other reason which takes me out of the country.'

It is clear that having and using personal ties and connections are a necessity for doing business. It is also clear that the underlying principles of this practice are reciprocity and the *quid pro quo* of business and social exchange.[6] The question that immediately arises is how do foreign organizations and businessmen fit in this framework? If the foreign organization does not have the necessary ties or connections, it is very likely that a national (local) agent or middleman would have to be used.

The use of agents or middlemen evokes the topic of commissions and bribery: a very delicate and controversial topic. To start with, it seems that bribery and other corrupt practices are world-wide phenomena. Reports of corruption involving individuals and organizations are common in the leading industrialized countries. On the individual level, for example, these reports cover corrupt practices by a variety of people including police commissioners, elected and non-elected politicians and so on. On the organizational level, there was an upsurge recently in reports of corruption by organizations engaged in business, especially in overseas business.[7] The six Arab countries included in this study are no exception. It is not the intention here, however, to raise questions regarding the extent and magnitude of corrupt practices in the Arab world *vis-à-vis* other countries; what functions/purpose, if any, these practices serve; what value standards we use to judge the immorality or morality of these practices. These and other questions are beyond the scope of this study.[8]

The pertinent question for present purposes is: what are the relationships between personal ties/connections and middlemen/agents. To the Arab business mind, using personal ties and connections, because of their reciprocal nature, means using up old 'credits' or accumulating new 'liabilities' depending on one's 'balance sheet' of reciprocal transactions. Either way, there is usually a value attached to the use of personal connections which is not always an economic value. Now, when a foreign organization employs an agent or a middleman to act on its behalf, the agent/middleman will incur several costs, one of which might be the cost of capital; his personal ties/connections 'capital'. For these services the agent/middleman feels entitled to a commission. Thus, while there is one line between commissions and bribery for the Westerner doing business in the Arab world, the dividing line may be drawn differently for the Arab middleman. The line of demarcation to the Arab is a clear one. He may or may not use a portion of his commission for bribery; but for him the commission represents a fee for services rendered. This is how one Arab businessman differentiated between corruption and commission:

> If one offers money to a government to influence it, that is corruption. But if someone receives money for services rendered afterwards, that is a commission.[9]

When asked about the closely related subject of giving and taking gifts, most of the Arab executives interviewed indicated that token gifts are 'normal' and 'acceptable'. They placed token gifts in the same category as other acts of hospitality such as business entertainment and/or receiving business guests at the airport.[10] They explained that such gifts when exchanged by businessmen are considered as mementoes of friendship and association. If, however, they are heavily one-sided, or greatly unequal in value, or given with the purpose of inducing favourable treatment, then such 'gifts' may become bribery.

In brief, bribery and the use of personal ties and connections have roots not only in the social structure and its institutions, but are also influenced by the value system of that society. Fayerweather viewed it as a societal decision involving the society's value system.

> The choice is between an irregular and personalized method of administration and a systematized and impersonal approach. In the United States there is tremendous emphasis on regularizing and systematizing life in the interests of efficiency and maximum productivity. By contrast, in many foreign countries these objectives receive far less weight and, given the individualistic approach to life along with the low pay of government workers, the exchange of bribes for special treatment does not meet with the same disapproval.[11]

It is worthwhile to reiterate here that while many of the executives viewed with disfavour the use of personal ties and connections, it is often their only viable alternative. As we have pointed out, both society's values and its formal institutions strongly encourage the use of these 'irregular and personalized' methods of doing business.

THE IMPORTANCE OF LOYALTY

We have seen in the preceding chapters that loyalty and trust are of paramount importance in Arab society. When the three types of Arab communities (tribal, rural and urban) were examined, it was pointed out that loyalty is a highly valued personality trait which is considered essential to the solidarity of tribes, clans and families. Additionally, there are strong societal norms and expectations which regard nepotism as natural and acceptable. Finally, we have seen that the majority of Arab executives view their organizations as family units, often assuming a paternal role in them.

In view of the above findings, we set out to investigate the attitudes of Arab executives towards employee loyalty. To what extent do executives value employee loyalty within their organizations? Is employee loyalty more highly valued than, for instance, employee efficiency? The executives were asked to rank the importance of loyalty and efficiency. The following questions were asked:

1. 'The ideal employee would be, among other things, both loyal and efficient. But unfortunately this does not always occur. In such cases, then, which would you prefer – to have *employees* in your company who are (a) more loyal to the company, *or* (b) more efficient on the job?'
2. 'What about your preference concerning your own immediate subordinate – would you prefer your *immediate subordinate* to be (a) more loyal to you, *or* (b) more efficient in his work?'

TABLE 6.2 Executives' preference for loyalty and efficiency

	(a) Employee		(b) Immediate Subordinate	
	Loyalty	Efficiency	Loyalty	Efficiency
Number	35	17	37	15
Percentage	67	33	71	29

The results show that executives valued loyalty more highly than efficiency for both employees in general, Table 6.2(a), and for their immediate subordinates, Table 6.2(b). Before we discuss the implications of these findings, let us briefly examine the relationship between the executives' responses and other organizational or individual variables. As mentioned earlier in Chapter 4, data were collected on a variety of variables such as country, size, age, nature of business and ownership of the organization; the age, occupational status, educational and social background of the executive.

Starting with Table 6.2(a) and using χ^2 tests, we find that executives' responses are significantly related to only one of the above variables: educational background. Executives with exposure to Western university education ($N=26$) were equally divided (50 per cent) between employee loyalty and efficiency. While 85 per cent of the executives without exposure to Western university education ($N=26$) preferred loyalty to efficiency ($\chi^2=7.08$; df=1; $p<0.01$). Those executives who were exposed to Western education did so by obtaining either their undergraduate, graduate, or postgraduate (Ph.D.) degrees from Western universities; while the executives without exposure to Western education either had no university degrees or held degrees from Arab universities. It seems that some of the Western-educated executives have been influenced by Western educational curricula as well as by Western norms, both of which emphasize efficiency at the organizational level.

Turning to Table 6.2(b), we find that the executives' preferences between loyalty and efficiency of their *immediate subordinate* are also significantly related to only one variable: the executive's occupational status, that is whether he is an owner/partner or a non-owner/partner. Of those executives who owned or partly owned their organizations ($N=29$), 86 per cent preferred loyalty of immediate subordinate over efficiency; while 52 per cent of the non-owners ($N=23$) felt that way ($\chi^2=7.35$; df=1; $p<0.01$). In this case, where immediate subordinates are concerned, the executives' ownership stake in the organization overshadows any influence which Western exposure and education may have had on their attitudes towards efficiency and loyalty.

Tables 6.2 (a and b) show that over two-thirds of Arab executives rank loyalty higher than efficiency for all levels of employees. The attributes of loyalty and efficiency as used in this section are meant to serve as indicators of person-orientation and task-orientation respectively. Thus loyalty with its connotation of trust and faithfulness emphasizes the person more than the task; while efficiency with its connotation of capability and competence puts more emphasis on the task and the ability to get the work done. The implication for personnel selection can be summarized by this typical statement mentioned by some of the executives: 'If the employee is loyal we can always train him and improve his efficiency.' In short, the attitude of 'loyalty first, efficiency second' within organizations seems to be in accordance with the larger societal values of group loyalty, nepotism, and paternalism.

AN OPEN-DOOR TRADITION

Another deeply-rooted tradition that found its way into today's Arab organizations is the open-door policy. In some countries in the Arabian peninsula it is still possible for any national to walk into the sheikh's, ruler's, or king's *majlis* (assembly or visiting room) where the visitor can either pay his respects, or request a favour, or submit a grievance.[12] While it is easier for the ruler to control the frequency and timing of his *majlis* meetings, the Arab executive will probably find it harder to do so with his employees.

How widespread is this open-door tradition? Table 6.3 summarizes the responses of the executives concerning this tradition. It must be noted that many of the executives who believed in the unconditional open-door policy (75 per cent of all executives), hastily added that their employees come to them with two different types of problems or requests. The first type consists of work-related problems or requests in which case the executive, having listened to the problems, will usually refer the employee back to his immediate manager or supervisor. The second type is when the employee has a personal problem or request. Here, the executive may either refer the employee to the personnel department or he may himself get involved, depending on the nature of the problem or request. We have seen earlier in Chapter 3, that handling the personal problems of employees is an accepted and expected part of the executive's role. The open-door tradition facilitates the playing of that role. Viewed in this context, the open-door tradition is an integral part of the 'unwritten' or 'informal' organizational structure.

TABLE 6.3 The open-door tradition

Level of employees who can meet the executive	Number	Percentage
1. Any level of the company, without going through hierarchy	39	75
2. Any level, provided they go through proper hierarchy	9	17
3. Managerial level only	3	6
4. Immediate subordinates only	1	2
Total	52	100

There were, however, thirteen executives (25 per cent) who were trying to discourage the open-door tradition, most of whom insisted that their employees must go through the established chain of command; a conditional open-door policy (see Table 6.3). A relevant question here would be whether there is any relationship between the open-door tradition and the other variables especially, as one would suspect, the size of the organization, the country, or the social and educational background of the executive? Surprisingly, the executives' responses were not related to any organizational or individual variables. What these thirteen executives shared in common was a desire to break away, within their respective organizations, from a tradition which they perceived as an unnecessary imposition on their energy and time. To that extent, these executives can be regarded as agents of social change, whether or not they are aware of the consequences of their actions.

It would be interesting to see how often Arab executives bypass their subordinates when issuing instructions to employees at the middle or lower levels.

It is clear from Table 6.4 that the executives were more careful about bypassing the hierarchy. Again, as with the preceding responses, there were no significant relationships between the executives' responses and the various variables. It is noteworthy, however, that most of the thirteen executives who favoured either conditional open-door or closed-door policies were relatively consistent in their attitudes towards bypassing the hierarchy. Eight of the thirteen said that they 'seldom' break the chain of command, and the remaining five indicated that they do so 'occasionally'. The executives were aware of the inevitable dilemma they face when deciding whether or not to break the chain of command. On the one hand, if they choose not to bypass subordinates they will encounter two disadvantages. The first is the loss of valuable time when the matters under consideration are urgent. The second disadvantage concerns communication; the ways in which communication can become distorted when flowing up and down the hierarchical levels are well known. On the other hand, if the executives decide to break the chain of command they will again face two disadvantages. One is the detrimental effects on the morale and effectiveness of their middle managers who are being bypassed. The other disadvantage is the bad example and precedent which actions of this kind could create for employees. One executive described it well when he said: 'We are having a hard time as it is getting our employees accustomed to organization charts and job descriptions. What will happen if I go around breaking these rules?' The solution to this dilemma rests with each executive who has to weigh the advantages and disadvantages of each alternative, taking into account the situational factors that led to the dilemma in the first place.

TABLE 6.4   Bypassing the hierarchy.

'*How often do you personally give instructions to employees at the middle or lower levels without going through their immediate supervisors?*'

	Number	Percentage
Very often	5	10
Occasionally	25	48
Seldom	22	42
Total	52	100

A PREFERENCE FOR 'INFORMALITY'

We have seen in the preceding sections that Arab executives tend to be more person-oriented that role- or task-oriented. They engage in prolonged rituals when starting a business discussion; they use personal ties and connections extensively; they value loyalty over efficiency; and they adhere to the open-door tradition. This strong emphasis on personal relations and the human side of business may seem incompatible with the rationale of formal organizational structures, rules and systems. In other words, the personal relationships within an organization often take precedence over formal structures, rules and procedures, and so on. The formal systems, being very fluid and elastic, are often used as tentative guidelines to action if and when necessary or convenient.

The above situation is best illustrated if seen through Western eyes. To an expatriate manager who has never worked in an Arab organization, the first few months at his new assignment may be traumatic. This is not so much due to the expected culture shock, but more to the manner in which his new organization functions. One such expatriate was given upon arrival an elaborate set of manuals which included company policies and procedures, job descriptions, and organization charts. Being in a relatively large public company (around 2500 employees), the expatriate expected that the formal rules and regulations would be applied most of the time. His comments were:

> I can now say that rules and regulations are being applied about 20% of the time. Not that they are not suitable for this type of firm; the problem is that we have too many exceptions around here: exceptions because of friendship, exceptions for relatives, exceptions because of convenience, etc. . . .

A similar phenomenon was observed by Riggs when studying public administration organizations.[13] He noted that in societies where partial differentiation has taken place (that is developing countries), there is great discrepancy between the formally prescribed laws and procedures and the actual behaviour of government officials. A study of Saudi Arabian bureaucracy, using the conceptual model developed by Riggs, has added further support to this observation.[14] To a non-Arab, such situations as described above will seem chaotic and unorganized. The expatriate (and to some extend the researcher) is bewildered at the discrepancy between organizational rules and procedures and the actual behaviour of top and middle level managers. Another expatriate who joined a large Arab organization at the vice-presidential level described his initial experience as follows:

> After the first three months I was convinced that the company was run in the most chaotic way imaginable; nothing like I ever experienced in my 20 years of work experience in the United States. But, now after nine months, I must admit these fellows are sharp, shrewd and efficient. . . . What they have is organized chaos and if you can adjust to that, it's a great place to work.

What are the Arab executive's views on this topic? Once again the executive is in a dilemma on this matter. He recognizes the benefits of formal rules and procedures especially as his firm increases in size and complexity: a well-organized firm has a better chance of increased productivity and effectiveness. But he is constantly faced with overwhelming pressures to use impersonal and irregular ways and means of getting business done, both in and out of the organization. He strives for more formalization, often by emulating those formal organizational methods used by non-Arab companies or those prescribed by non-Arab management textbooks. However, these more formalized structures and methods are necessarily impersonal and universalistic[15] and as we have seen earlier, society's values and its institutions do not encourage the use of such impersonal methods.

Of course, Arab executives do use and adhere to formal rules and regulations whenever possible or legally required. But the majority of them seemed to favour keeping formal methods to the *minimum* required by legal, accounting, contractual and other necessary procedures. They also favoured keeping to a minimum the formality of interpersonal relations, stating that with informality a 'personal' and a 'humane' management approach is more possible; an approach which they seem to value highly, and which is consistent with both the executive's and the employee's perception of their organization as a family unit.

What is particularly interesting is the Arab executive's informality in decision making. We have already seen that the executives prefer the consultative style of decision making. This consultation is usually carried out on a person-to-person basis whereby group meetings are strongly avoided. Moreover, decisions are often made in an informal and unstructured manner, as one European expatriate discovered early on in his career with a large oil company in the UAE:

> It took me several months to realize that what looked and sounded like social talk and playing around was in fact the most preferred mode for Arab managers to discuss business, solve problems, or make decisions.

Another indication that Arab executives prefer informality and the personal approach to business can be seen from their views about expatriates and/or foreign businessmen. When asked to mention the characteristics of expatriates/foreign businessmen which they strongly disliked, nine executives mentioned the formal and impersonal notion of 'business is business' which they felt was carried too far by expatriates/foreign businessmen.[16] In a society where the personalized approach is prevalent, it is not surprising that what is normally considered professional business behaviour was seen as highly rigid and impersonal. This is not to say that Arab executives do not believe in the notion of 'business is business', it is only that they feel business should be conducted in a personalized and friendly atmosphere – even though this may require 'a lot of play-acting', as one of the executives put it.

In conclusion, the discussion presented in this chapter points to a strong preference by the Arab executive for a person-oriented approach to interpersonal relations. This was evident not only when the executive was dealing with people from outside his organization, but also with his employees. In turn this approach led to its corollary: a preference for 'informality'. This type of behaviour is partly shaped by social structural factors and partly by the prevailing customs and value orientations. It is significant to note, however, that there were some executives who consciously or unconsciously were striving for more impersonality and formality in conducting business. This suggests that the differences in approaches may well be reflections of the social changes now taking place in the Arab world: a topic we shall focus on in the next chapter.

NOTES

1. This range of 2 to 15 minutes is based on estimates given by sixteen executives from the six Arab countries. The average time for this ritual was 5.7 minutes and the mode was 5 minutes.
2. Morris (1967), *The Naked Ape*, p. 180.
3. Hall and Whyte, 'Intercultural Communication', pp. 5–12.
4. Six expatriates were interviewed and their opinions were solicited regarding Arab executives.
5. The importance of the intermediary role in Egyptian civil service was described over twenty years ago by Berger (1957), in *Bureaucracy and Society in Modern Egypt*. For the importance of this role in Lebanon, see Farsoun (1970), 'Family Structure and Society in Modern Lebanon', pp. 270, 281–5.
6. For an excellent analysis of social exchange, see Homans (1961), *Social Behavior*; or Blau (1964), *Exchange and Power in Social Life*.
7. See for example, 'Bribery, Corruption, or Necessary Fees and Charges?' *Multinational Business* 3 (1975), pp. 1–17; Jacoby et al. (1977), *Bribery*

INTERPERSONAL STYLE 87

    and Extortion in World Business. For a vivid account of bribery in the arms industry, see Sampson (1977), *The Arms Bazaar*.
8. For an excellent collection of articles and studies on these questions, and on world-wide corruption, see Heidenheimer (1971), *Political Corruption: Readings in Comparative Analysis*, especially Part 4 on Corruption and Modernization, pp. 479–578.
9. As quoted in Sampson (1977), p. 189.
10. Business guests in the Arab world are often treated in the same individualized manner as would heads of state visiting other countries – but of course on a lesser scale and without the paraphernalia.
11. Fayerweather (1960), *Management of International Operations*, p. 27.
12. Hobday (1978), *Saudi Arabia Today*, pp. 67–8. It was at one such *majlis* where the late King Faisal was assassinated in March 1975.
13. Riggs (1964), *Administration in Developing Countries*.
14. Al-Awaji (1971), 'Bureaucracy and Society in Saudi Arabia', Ph.D. diss., University of Virginia.
15. Universalistic as contrasted to particularistic; the classic examples of the latter are nepotism and other forms of favouritism; see Parsons (1966), *Societies: Evolutionary and Comparative Perspectives*.
16. These views were in response to an open-ended question which also asked executives to mention the characteristics which they *admire* most about expatriates/foreign businessmen. The responses to both these questions will be examined in the next two chapters.

7 Attitudes Towards Time and Change

> Time present and time past
> Are both perhaps present in time future
> And time future contained in time past.
> T.S. Eliot, 1888–1965
> 'Burnt Norton', *Four Quartets*

A study of the Arab executive would be incomplete and inadequate without examining his attitudes towards time and change. For these are two crucial elements of the business mind which, in turn, have significant bearing on managerial behaviour and practices, including business activities at the international level.

In the first part of this chapter, the time orientation of the Arab executive will be examined. Here we focus on the value the executive places on time, his time horizons; and his attitudes towards the future. The second part will investigate the executive's views on the technological and social changes which are now permeating his organization and his society. Finally, the last part will examine the socio-psychological consequences to the executive of these recent changes, particularly the recent rush towards economic development and modernization.

TIME ORIENTATION

Because of its importance to the understanding of human nature and behaviour, the time orientation of man has interested social scientists especially in their endeavour to understand human behaviour in societies other than their own.[1] In the following sections our interest goes further than presenting a description of the executive's time orientation, for we shall also attempt to identify the environmental and social structural factors which are at present influencing the executive's time orientation. Viewed from this perspective, time orientation ceases to be a mere static cultural trait or value pattern, instead it will be viewed both as a product of early socialization and enculturation as well as a product of an ever-changing social structure.

The Value of Time

One of the Arab executive's gravest problems is the low value placed on time by many of his countrymen. Executives were deeply concerned and irritated by the lack of appreciation towards time shown by people with whom they come in contact. The seriousness of this problem was perhaps best expressed by the motto of a large firm in the UAE. Above and across the main entrance of its building there is written in huge letters the following: 'WASTE EVERYTHING EXCEPT TIME'.

We have already seen in Chapter 3 that Arab executives considered procrastination and the low value placed on time as a major problem in their society. In fact this problem was the most frequently mentioned and was seen as such by nineteen executives (see Chapter 3, Table 3.1). The executives' profound concern with the value of time is also reflected in their responses to the following question: 'what are some of the characteristics of the expatriates employed here (if no expatriates, then foreign businessmen) which you admire most?' The admired characteristic which again was the most frequently mentioned (eighteen executives mentioned it) is the expatriate's punctuality and respect for time.

In view of the above, it was not suprising to find that executives placed a very high value on time; at least when asked to provide proverbs or sayings that would best represent their views and attitudes towards time. The results are presented in Table 7.1. Clearly, the executives value time highly. However, cognizant of the fact that the above responses are only views and attitudes and as such are not necessarily indicative of actual behaviour, the author attempted to uncover the precise meaning which executives attach to these proverbs. In other words, could this high value placed on time possibly be an overreaction to the widespread general indifference and apathy towards time? Or is it an aspiration and a goal on the part of the executives for more appreciation of time? Where do executives draw the line when they say 'time is money'? The discussions and the probing that took place indicate that the degree and extent to which time is valued may differ from other non-Arab societies. Thus while time is highly valued by Arab executives there seem to be several other competing factors which often take precedence over time. For example, one executive said: 'It is unethical to say to an unexpected guest or visitor: "Sorry I've an appointment or urgent work".' Similarly, it is difficult for the executive to shorten a guest's visit even though the executive's work load justifies doing so. In such cases, both the norms of hospitality and deference to others preclude time-saving actions. Other competing factors are friendship and personal ties. Here, again, executives were aware that while time is spent in seemingly non-productive activities, they viewed time thus spent as an investment in friendships and personal ties – both highly valued elements – whether or not future benefits are forthcoming. Finally, a few executives indicated that while they believe that 'time is money' or 'gold', one must temper this attitude whenever human relations and personal problems are involved. It was a Saudi executive, with extensive exposure to US management and personnel, who succinctly summarized the views of many Arab executives: 'While Arabs, unfortunately, have little respect for time, the Americans go to the other extreme ... there must be a happy medium'.

TABLE 7.1 Proverbs on the value of time

Proverb	Frequency of mention*
1 Time is gold (translated from Arabic)	14 ⎱ 24
2 Time is money (mentioned in English)	10 ⎰
3 Time is like a double-edged sword, it could either benefit or harm you (translated from Arabic)	8
4 Don't postpone today's work till tomorrow (translated from Arabic); which is similar to the English: 'Never put off till tomorrow what may be done today'.	6
5 Time is a problem solver (translated from Arabic)	4

*A total of eleven proverbs were mentioned; the six proverbs which do not appear above were mentioned only once.

Let us very briefly summarize the probable pressures and reasons which inhibit a better utilization of time in the Arab world. Some of the following may in other societies be considered as easily avoidable constraints on time but are seen by

ATTITUDES TOWARDS TIME AND CHANGE 91

Arab executives as either necessary or uncontrollable:

1. The inadequacy of the economic and organizational infrastructures was discussed in Chapter 2. Here, delays and waste of time are often a result of the non-existence and/or poor utilization of such items as transportation, housing facilities, communication channels, technology, and human resources, or efficient government agencies.
2. A range of social pressures and constraints impose on the executive's time. They include: fusion of business, social, and personal life; top-man syndrome; and social visits at the office (see Table 3.1, Chapter 3).
3. The executive's role in the community and the organization, as we have seen in Chapter 3, resulted in heavy time commitments and obligations to the extended family, friends, and employees.
4. The low level of delegation by executives, as was discovered in Chapter 4, is an obstacle to good management of time. Here the onus is on the executives themselves. Clearly delegating more of the operating-level decisions will, *inter alia*, relieve the over-burdened executive and speed up the decision-making process.
5. The executives' person-oriented interpersonal style, discussed in Chapter 6, was partly imposing on their time; especially with executives who use the Arab rituals and customs while conducting business, and with those who believe in the open-door tradition.

These constraints could have detrimental effects on attempts to manage one's time. It must be pointed out, however, that throughout this study an effort was made to highlight those few executives who were actively resisting the social and structural constraints on their time, energy, and behaviour. Those executives were, on several occasions, termed agents of change. The main point is this: the executive may indeed have a choice. Clearly, it is not an easy choice; the price of non-conformity may be too high for some executives.

Time Horizons

How far into the future do Arab executives attempt to glimpse or predict? And to what extent do political and economic factors influence their time horizons? These questions become even more crucial if we keep in mind the instability and unpredictability of political and economic conditions in the Arab world. There are strong indications that executives, given these adverse conditions, nevertheless project their business plans well into the future. In order to find out the extent to which they do that, the executives were asked to indicate their time horizon on three preselected business activities: capital investment; company-wide planning; and managerial training and development. Their responses were recorded on the time scale shown in Table 7.2. Additionally, comments on these activities were solicited from executives whenever their time permitted. The responses and some of the comments will be briefly outlined here, while the implications of these results will be discussed in the following section.

TABLE 7.2   Time horizons: investment, planning, training

Time period (years)	Payback on capital investment	Company-wide planning	Managerial training and development
Under 1	1	7	14
1– 2	2	18	16
3– 5	30	25	19
6–10	14	2	3
Over 10	1	–	–
Total	48*	52	52

* Four executives preferred not to respond, stating that their expectations on payback periods varied greatly depending on the nature and circumstances of individual projects.

The most interesting comments were related to company-wide planning. For in addition to the unstable and uncertain political and economic conditions (discussed in Chapter 2), the dearth of data and information was seen as a main obstacle to corporate planning. Business-related information and data in the Arab world are scarce resources; and if available they are, in the words of one executive, 'often inadequate, unreliable, and conflicting'. Under such conditions, the necessity to review and revise corporate plans on an annual basis becomes obvious, as many executives seem to be doing. Finally, since governmental expenditures have the greatest impact on the national economies, several executives utilize the three-, four-, or five-year economic development plans for their own corporate planning. Of course, executives in the government-owned organizations (there were twelve such executives) coordinate their long-term planning with the government's own 3–5-year development plan.

Only a brief comment is necessary on managerial training and development. At the one end of the scale (under 1 year), short training programmes are being utilized, ranging in duration from 1 week to several months. At the other extreme (3–10 years), executives from some organizations stated that 'a whole second generation of top men is at present being groomed for future leadership'; while other executives mentioned that their organizations pay for the university education of prospective managers.

The results on capital investment horizons demonstrate that Arab executives have generally the same time horizons as businessmen in some industrialized countries, as indicated by the following quotation:

> Surveys among businessmen almost invariably reveal that for judgements about the desirability of individual projects and for choices among projects the shortness of the payback period is a much more popular criterion than the other analytical criteria.... Some of these surveys disclose, indeed, that a surprising number of businesses set arbitrary payback period cutoffs, such as three, four, or five years, beyond which they will not go in making investments in new facilities.[2]

Table 7.2 shows that there were three organizations with payback periods of 2 years or less, and one organization with a period of over 10 years. The former organizations were all small (less than 500 employees) contracting companies, while the latter was a shipping firm whose capital investments are greater in magnitude and have longer economic lives.

The Myth of Fatalism

There is a widespread view which asserts that Arabs are fatalistic, and that this fatalism is in direct contrast with the spirit of activity and initiative said to be characteristic of Anglo-Saxons and Europeans. Furthermore, this view attributes this fatalistic indifference to the teachings of Islam.[3]

The aim of this section is not to engage in a delicate and philosophical debate concerning the relationships between the revelational religions (Judaism, Christianity, and Islam) and fatalism – a topic beyond the scope of this book. Instead, our aim is to highlight the findings of this study which cast serious doubt on the above view held mostly by Western social scientists. More specifically, there are two objections to this view:

1. That the degree of fatalism in the Arab world – and there are degrees of fatalism – must not be attributed solely to Islam without taking into account all other socio-economic and political factors. Moreover, that there are within Islamic teachings as many precepts exhorting initiative, activity, and reasoning as there are precepts which encourage fatalism.
2. That, as a corollary to the above, any generalization which implies that *most* Arabs (Muslim or non-Muslim) are fatalistic, regardless of their socio-economic and educational background, is academically irresponsible and misleading.

Let us now turn to the first point. The view which attributes fatalism to Islam is not a new one. Rodinson (1974) writes:

> This view is, as is well known, one of the most widespread held about Islam in Europe, and has even acquired the status of an established truth, a dogma for the European collective mind, well expressed in Leibniz's expression *fatum mahumetanum*. It was developed by innumerable European writers in the eighteenth and nineteenth centuries.... It is still frequently repeated in our own time. And yet it is highly questionable. (p. 109)

The interest in the relationship between Islam and fatalism gained prominence when scholars attempted to explain the decline and prolonged stagnation of the Arab empire and Islamic civilization. In the majority of these investigations Islam – as a religion and a civilization – was being compared to Christian or European civilization *without* taking into account the historical, political, socio-economic, or geophysical factors.[4] Under these circumstances, that is, ahistorical and non-specific analyses, 'it was perhaps inevitable that Islam itself should emerge as the fundamental reason why the East has not developed in the same way as the West'.[5] It was in this type of analysis that the alleged fatalism was ascribed to Islamic teachings and hence was held responsible for the general stagnation.

To confound matters, the social scientists studying this topic focused their attention mostly on the rural areas of the Islamic countries, generalizing from there to all Muslims. To quote Rodinson (1974) again:

> The examples of 'Muslim fatalism' that have probably been most often quoted by European writers were taken above all from the under-developed *rural areas* of the Islamic world. G. Destanne de Bernis has shown in a very scholarly way, using mathematical methods and with a close and deep knowledge of the Tunisian *country life*, that, if the peasants of the Muslim countries are indeed fatalistic, this is not at all an irrational attitude on their part, but represents a just estimation of the enormous, and discouraging, weight of the chancy factors that condition the success of their efforts. (p. 113, emphasis added)

With regard to Islamic precepts exhorting initiative, activity and reasoning, it would be relatively easy to quote verses from the Quran and the *Hadīth* in order to illustrate Islam's rationalist and activist teachings.[6] It would be equally easy to quote verses which can be interpreted as fatalistic.[7] For our present purpose, it suffices to report what some Arab executives had to say on this topic. Three of the executives reminded the author of a saying from the *Hadīth* which in effect admonishes man first to think and plan ahead, then put his trust in God. Another executive quoted the following verse from the Quran: 'Verily never will God change the condition of a people until they change it themselves.'[8] The fifth executive stated his belief that 'Man's trust in God or belief in God's will does not necessarily mean a curb on human will . . . man must strive to do his best and if he acts rightly God will be with him; I don't believe that this leads to passive resignation.'

Indeed, past and present Islamic achievements (which are in harmony with Islamic teachings) demonstrate the use of long-range planning and a desire to understand and control nature or the environment. These include, to name a few examples, empire building in the past and economic development today; the utilization of technological, scientific, and medical know-how; and the advancement of knowledge through education and research. None of these indicates a belief that man cannot or should not shape his future. And yet these are the goals and aspirations of many devout Muslim nations and/or individuals.

Let us now consider the second point, namely, the insinuation that most Arabs are fatalistic. This usually stems from the argument we have just discussed alleging that Islam encourages fatalism. By association, since 90–95 per cent of Arabs are Muslims, it is erroneously implied that most Arabs are fatalistic. This may well have been the case many decades ago when poverty and ignorance were widespread, especially in the rural areas of the Arab world. Today, modern agricultural technology and methods are widely used; bedouins and peasants seek medical attention (even if abroad);[9] agricultural cooperatives and banks are widespread, and so on. Again, none of these activities suggest a belief that man should not seek self-betterment or should not influence future events. However, it is perhaps the frequent use by Arabs of the phrase *insha'Allāh* (God willing or if God wills) which alarms expatriates and foreign visitors. But instead of interpreting it as a sign of resignation and inactivity, one must consider it a sign of religiousness and/or religious custom which most often it is. One is reminded of the phrase 'In God We Trust' which appears on US coin and note currencies; or the Christian Lord's Prayer: 'Give us this day our daily bread'; or the expression of shock and sadness upon the untimely death of Pope John Paul I in September 1978 as expressed in these quotations: 'God has willed it, as painful as His will is', or 'The Ways of the Lord are disconcerting to our human perspective'.[10]

Turning to the Arab executive's attitudes toward this subject, we find that he is not only future-orientated but also takes as many preventive measures against undesirable events as it is technologically and economically feasible. We have already seen in the preceding section that his time horizons extend to 10 years on capital investment, company-wide planning, and managerial training and development. The most common (mode) time period for these business activities being 3–5 years.

TABLE 7.3 Events and factors beyond the executive's control. (In open response.)

Event	Frequency of mention*
Adverse political and economic conditions (national and international)	33
Government rules and regulations (unstable or restrictive)	21
World currency fluctuation (especially in the dollar)	9
Manpower and labour shortage	7
Climatic conditions or natural disasters	6
Inflation	5
Delays with imported materials (at sending and receiving ends)	4

* Shows only events mentioned by three or more executives

Further data from the interviews strongly support the claim that Arab executives are not fatalistic. The executives were asked to mention the events and factors that have an effect on their business, but over which they have little control. Table 7.3 summarizes their responses. The seven items mentioned in Table 7.3 are self-explanatory except the first and most frequently mentioned one.[11] Executives combined political and economic events at both the national and international levels. The most prominent examples were: world-wide recession and market conditions; regional and internal wars and border closures; and local economic instability and uncertainty. The executives were also asked whether they take steps or measures to prevent undesirable events from occuring in the course of doing business. Their responses are shown in Table 7.4.[12]

TABLE 7.4 Preventive measures. (In open response.)

Measures	Frequency of mention*
Contingency planning (plan ahead)	30†
Safety	27
Preventive maintenance	18
Insurance (on plant and/or personnel)	13
Maintaining good labour and employee relations	6

* Shows only measures mentioned by three or more executives.
† Includes six executives who specifically mentioned spare parts planning.

Finally, executives were asked if they carry life insurance and if not, why not. Twenty-nine executives (56 per cent) have life insurance, while the other twenty-three (44 per cent) did not. The reasons given by those who did not have life insurance are interesting and worth looking into. Of the twenty-three executives, sixteen said they did not need life insurance because of their individual or family wealth and financial security; and five of those sixteen stated that in the past they had insurance but could not see a need for it now. Of the remaining seven executives, four said they did not feel that they need life insurance since their countries' (Kuwait and Saudi Arabia) social security systems, as well as their company's pension and benefit plans, are very generous and thus adequate. The other three executives simply stated that they do not believe in its financial benefits or its usefulness, without elaborating further.[13]

In brief, the data we have presented indicate that Arab executives are far from being fatalistic: they are future-oriented, rational in their planning and deliberation, and they attempt to control and prevent adverse future events.

From our brief exploration of this important issue, it would seem that the myth of fatalism, at least among businessmen, must now be laid to rest. Any future investigation of this topic should not only seek objectively to assess the degree and extent of fatalism, but also take into account the relevant historical and contextual variables. In this way, we can not only compare the degrees of fatalism within a given society, but we can also compare fatalism across different societies.

ATTITUDES TOWARDS CHANGE

In the remainder of this chapter, we focus on the Arab executive's attitudes and reactions to social and technological change. The understanding of these attitudes and reactions is of great importance since the executive himself is a target of change; and as we have seen throughout this study, he could also be an agent of change. It is equally important, however, that we discuss the executive's attitudes and reactions to change within a specific background: that of change and modernization at the national level. The next few pages will thus provide a context for the following discussions.

The Context of Change

There is no doubt that many changes are taking place in the Arab world. In Chapter 2 we discussed at the macro-level several major events which are still influencing every aspect of life in the region. Clearly, the pace and intensity of these changes differ from one country to another. Moreover, internal as well as external developments and forces are inducing the changes since none of the countries is in complete isolation.

There are, however, two types of change.[14] Stated simply, one type refers to the minor, and in the short run, insignificant changes that are continuously occurring *within* society and its social structure. When such changes occur, the structure and the values and norms of society do not change substantially. A good example would be the introduction of modern technology to replace the old. The use of modern communication and information systems (telephone, telex, computers and so on) by governmental, military, or business organizations are changes in methods but not in basic structures. Examples of such changes abound: changes in national dress, diet, housing, entertainment, or medical practices. However, these changes are taking place *within* the social structure, and may not be cumulative or sufficient to induce lasting structural or normative changes.

The second type of change involves fundamental and substantive shifts in a society's social structure, its institutions, or in its values and norms. This type of change may take place either gradually, as a result of the cumulative effects of the minor changes discussed above; or more abruptly as a reaction to crises and major historical events. Either way, the form and functions of the social structure or some of its institutions change dramatically. Again, the change may well be in one or more of its political, military, religious, economic, or family institutions. Specific examples of such fundamental changes include: major shifts in power centres or in societal values which could result from political or social revolutions; the discovery and exploitation of natural resources, such as oil, in a previously impoverished country; a shift from the extended family to a nuclear one; and generally, a greater degree of differentiation in the political, economic, or social systems of a society.

The Arab world is experiencing *both* types of change; but

perhaps more of the first than the second. While changes are overwhelming in countries like Kuwait, Saudi Arabia, and the UAE, fuelled by the rapid increase in wealth; the social structure and most of its institutions have not changed drastically. Modernization and industrialization are taking place but within, more or less, the same traditional, political, religious, economic, or social systems.

It would be absurd, of course, to suggest that there is no conflict or tension between the old and the modern. It would be equally absurd, however, to argue that the old and the modern are diametrically opposed and hence completely incompatible; or to suggest that the evolutionary path to modernization must inevitably lead to a Western type of modernity.[15] This school of thought, referred to as the convergence school, measured societies on Western modernity indices which included (depending on the social scientist's field of interest) such items as literacy, fatalism, empathy, media participation, urbanization, political participation, division of labour, and the like. Nearly all the work done by adherents of this school theorized that 'modernizing' societies go from the 'traditional' stage through an intermediate 'transitional' stage on their way to more or less a Western 'modern' stage. And that in this modernization process the incompatible traditional values and institutions will ultimately disappear.

However, reality and systematic studies have not fully borne out these theories or their assumptions.[16] Riggs, among many others, has shown that the modern and the traditional can and do coexist in what he called the 'prismatic society' which is neither traditional nor Western-type modern,[17] and that the resultant partially differentiated society may be a viable alternative. Others have shown that tradition and modernity can be mutually reinforcing rather than in conflict, as has been found in field studies from Lebanon, Nigeria, and Indonesia.[18] A case study of Saudi Arabia supports these important findings:

> In conclusion, we find that modernization proceeds in degrees and stages. It does not have a uniform impact on the total structure of traditional societies. Whether it proceeds at first on the economic, the social, or the political level is determined by the national goals of the country concerned, given the limitations set by internal and external forces. *Moderniza-*

tion does not necessarily entail destruction of traditional structures, but rather it allows for 'wide margins' of coexistence between traditional and modern forms. On the other hand, tradition does not constitute a uniform, static system that is *antagonistic* to modernity. Tradition was found to have a significant degree of flexibility and diversity to *accommodate* modern patterns.[19] (Emphasis added)

Critical evaluations of the convergence school have been many,[20] and their criticisms fairly consistent: mainly that these studies ignore the viable mixture of traditional and modern elements as often found in contemporary societies, and that 'the mixture of the two types is too situational and historical to be consistent with the evolutionary theory which posits them as opposites'.[21] The author of the study on Saudi Arabia reached the same conclusion:

> Modernization is thus a continuing process in which the cultural and historical experience, and the national goals of the country concerned interfere to set their 'choice' of the margins of co-existence between tradition and modernity.[22]

It is perhaps with such thoughts in mind that the late King Faisal of Saudi Arabia declared in 1974 that he wanted his country 'to achieve economic growth and modernization without sacrificing the traditions of Islam and Arab culture'. He may have at that time set the tone for the Gulf states, but recent events in Egypt, Pakistan, and especially Iran, seem to indicate that Islam is also asserting its identity in other Muslim countries.[23] History and systematic studies have shown that modernization can be achieved under the tutelage of a variety of competing political, economic, or religious ideologies and systems. Indeed, modernization does not inevitably have to be of the Western type. Let us take, for example, the following countries and ask ourselves what must be included in a traditional/modern index for comparative purposes: USA, Japan, USSR, Italy, and Sweden. There is a great variety in their political, economic, social, and religious ideologies and systems. What is most common among them is the extensive usage of science and advanced technology for the production of goods and services.

In brief, it seems that a country could achieve economic

progress and could become modern in some but not all aspects of human activity. That is it could become neo-traditionalist: new and modern in form and style but not in substance or essence.[24]

The Executive's Attitudes

Now that the background has been set, let us turn to the Arab executive and examine his attitudes toward the technological and social changes which are now occurring within his milieu. Changes which he has some control over and hence could either promote or discourage, at least, within his organization and family. The executives were asked to express their attitudes towards three such changes:

1. an increase in the introduction of sophisticated scientific systems and equipment (computers, latest machinery, etc.) to business when and where applicable;
2. women holding high managerial positions in business firms;
3. the newer generation to gain more freedom and independence from family, customs, religion and traditions (for example, a move from the extended family to the nuclear one, and so on).

For convenience, let us abbreviate the wording of these changes and refer to them henceforth as follows:

1. advanced technology;
2. women in management;
3. freedom from family and traditions.

The responses, in their aggregate form, are summarized in Table 7.5. It is clear at once that Arab executives have a 'thirst' for technology; in fact some of these who only 'favoured' rather than 'strongly favoured' advanced technology admitted that they may well have been 'oversold' on its applicability. Nevertheless, introducing technological changes (where applicable) into Arab organizations is unlikely to meet resistance.

The second change, women in management, was also welcomed. In Chapter 3 we briefly discussed the societal restrictions on women, especially in Saudi Arabia and to a much lesser

TABLE 7.5 Attitudes towards technological and social changes (Percentages) (N=52)

Response	Advanced technology	Women in management	Freedom from family and traditions
Strongly favour	62	15	6
Favour	38	58	23
Oppose	—	21	40
Strongly oppose	—	6	31
Total	100	100	100

extent in Jordan. It was also stated that the trend towards female emancipation has accelerated in most Arab countries, possibly at a relatively faster rate than was the case for Western women some 50 years ago. It would be useful to take a closer look at the data. Table 7.6 shows, by country, the executives' attitudes towards women in management as well as the interesting responses on freedom from family and traditions.

TABLE 7.6 Attitudes towards social changes, by country (Percentages and mean scores)

Country	Women in management			Freedom from family and traditions			N
	Percentage		Mean score*	Percentage		Mean score*	
	Favour	Oppose		Favour	Oppose		
Jordan	90	10	3.1	40	60	2.4	10
Lebanon	63	37	2.5	63	37	2.7	8
Saudi Arabia	90	10	3.1	40	60	2.1	10
Kuwait	78	22	3.1	11	89	1.8	9
Egypt	44	56	2.4	11	89	1.6	9
UAE	67	33	2.5	—	100	1.5	6
Total	73	27	2.8	29	71	2.0	52

* The mean score is based on a four-point scale: 1 = strongly oppose; 2 = oppose; 3 = favour; and 4 = strongly favour. Thus, the higher the score the more favourable the attitude.

There are two noteworthy observations as suggested by the data. First, in regard to attitudes towards women in management, it seems that executives from those countries with lesser restrictions on women (Egypt and Lebanon) are least favourable to having women in managerial positions. This attitude is similar to the prevailing Western attitudes towards women 10 or 15 years ago. Although Egyptian women, especially in the urban areas, are holding high positions in politics, education, medicine, and social welfare, discrimination in industry and business continues. On the other hand, executives from the other four countries seem to be reacting strongly in response to what they see as the slower-than-desired process of women's emancipation in their respective countries.

The second observation relates to the reversal of attitudes from favouring women in management to opposing freedom from family and traditions. We must find out how many executives were involved in this attitude reversal; we can then look for possible explanations. Of the fifty-two executives:

(i) Fourteen executives (27 per cent) favoured both changes.
(ii) Thirteen executives (25 per cent) opposed both changes.
(iii) One executive (2 per cent) opposed women in management *but* favoured freedom from family and traditions.
(iv) Twenty-four executives (46 per cent) favoured women in management *but* opposed freedom from family and traditions.

Our primary interest is in those executives in (iii) and (iv) above. The one executive (in (iii)) is an Egyptian who, while favouring freedom from family and traditions, was opposed to women in management, an attitude not different from the one prevalent in the West not so long ago. Of the twenty-four executives (in (iv) above), twenty are from the same four countries (Jordan, Kuwait, Saudi Arabia and UAE) in which only recently did women's emancipation become an issue. The remaining four executives were from Egypt. One possible explanation for this seemingly ambivalent attitude is the belief that while more rights and opportunities for women is desirable, it is neither desirable nor inevitable for family ties and traditions to be weakened.[25] In other words, women's emancipation (especially in the management of business) is not seen as incompatible with

ATTITUDES TOWARDS TIME AND CHANGE

the maintenance of strong family ties and/or customs, religion and traditions. In short, as one executive put it: 'there is no need to go to the other extreme'.

Finally, it is worth noting that two executives from the Gulf area, after responding to the question on women in management, took the opportunity to comment on the subject of women's employment at all levels. Some pointed out that the acute manpower shortage in the Gulf area will be slightly alleviated if they utilize some of the 'womanpower surplus'. Of course, this has serious consequences for most of the Arab countries where the economically active population averages a low 26 per cent of the total population.[26]

What is the likelihood of each of the three changes occurring in the next 5-10 years? The executives' responses to this question are summarized in Table 7.7.

TABLE 7.7 Likelihood of occurrence: technological and social changes (Percentages) ($N=52$)

Response	Advanced technology	Women in management	Freedom from family and traditions
Very likely	63	17	10
Likely	37	40	67
Not likely	—	31	19
Highly unlikely	—	12	4
Total	100	100	100

Notice that while all three changes were seen by executives as likely to occur, the executives were opposed to only one of them; namely, freedom from family and tradition (see Table 7.5). A closer look at this incongruence reveals the following:

(i) Thirteen executives (25 per cent) favoured freedom from family and traditions, *and* believed it is likely to occur in the next 5-10 years.
(ii) Two executives (4 per cent) favoured *but* believed it is unlikely to occur.
(iii) Ten executives (19 per cent) opposed *and* believed it is unlikely to occur.
(iv) Twenty-seven executives (52 per cent) opposed *but* believed it is likely to occur.

Again, our interest is in the twenty-seven executives in (iv) above.[27] Further probing as to why they opposed the change and/or why they thought it was likely to happen brought three types of replies. First, there were those who felt that the new generation has already gained considerable freedom to which they were opposed. In these cases there already exists a generation gap. The second group felt that while they favour freedom in some customs and traditions, they oppose freedom in others – such as family or religion or vice versa. Clearly the question put to them was too general, thus suggesting the need to be more specific on this point in future research. Finally, the third group felt that while they favour a gradual change in these spheres of life, they wondered 'where does one draw the line?' Most were in effect saying it is 'unfortunate' but nevertheless likely that such a social change will occur *in the next 5–10 years.*

Our discussion of the executives' attitudes towards these three changes brings us back to the topic of 'convergence', and to the question of whether modernization will result in a 'mixture' of modern and traditional institutions and values. While political and social forces and events will mostly determine the outcome of such 'mixture', the executive's role in this process must not be understated, for he is still in a position to influence the composition and the ingredients which make up this 'mixture' of modern and traditional. However, the typical executive has ambivalent feelings towards modernization; a desire to avoid some of the negative consequences which might accompany economic development and modernization.

AMBIVALENCE

Modernization, perceived as a process whereby the old and the new ways of life mix and coexist, will invariably result in tension between the modern and the traditional. This tension is often manifested by ambivalent attitudes and emotions, especially by those persons most exposed to both modern and traditional. One such person is the Arab executive. He is torn between the old and the new; determined to introduce into his life and into his environment modern and scientific methods and adapt them to his modified, yet fundamentally traditional, work and life styles.

What is ambivalence? And how does it feel to have ambivalent attitudes, emotions, or behaviour? In its general sense, ambivalence means the coexistence in one person of opposing emotional attitudes towards the same object, or the simultaneous operation in the mind of two irreconcilable wishes. Examples of ambivalence abound, the many dilemmas and paradoxes of social life make ambivalence a more common phenomenon than is generally thought.[28] The classic example is of love and hate towards the same object, person, or situation (as in marriage, bringing up children, or even cigarette smoking). Other examples of ambivalence, whose sources are in the person's professional status and role, would include the ambivalence felt by physicians who were trained, and thus expected, to show sympathy as well as detachment towards patients; or the ambivalence of the scientists who feel obliged to publish quickly and to avoid rushing into print; to value humility as well as to take pride in originality.[29]

Yet the ambivalence felt by the Arab executive comes from an additional and different source: his exposure to the West. Of course, it was well before the executives in this study were born that the Arab world as a whole was reopened to the West. But the recent exposure of most executives has been considerable. Their educational backgrounds and the nature of their work made this exposure possible. For example 50 per cent of the executives received their first and/or second degree from Western universities. Another 20 per cent were educated at Western-styled universities (mostly at the American University of Beirut, but some at the American University of Cairo). These executives as well as all the others were also exposed to the West through one or more of the following: (a) extensive business and/or holiday travel in the industrialized countries; (b) short and intermediate (up to 1 year) training courses in the West; and (c) working closely with Western expatriates and businessmen.

The ambivalent feelings and attitudes of the executives are not unlike those felt by foreign students or immigrants who go to the West.[30] They see and experience the best and the worst of Western social order. They love the West for its many good features and they hate it for its many bad ones. When they return home, as in the case of foreign students, they begin to love even more than before their society's good points, but they start to hate the newly discovered bad ones. Most of them realize that a great deal has to be learnt now from the West, just as Europeans did from the Arabs a few centuries ago.

The solution for many of the executives is to adopt as many as possible of the West's good points which do not conflict with their own or society's values and norms. Whatever cannot be adopted is often adapted to fit in with the cherished traditional ways. At the same time, these executives attempt to discourage or curtail local habits and customs which they feel are hindering 'progress'. In one sense, the executives are searching for, and attempting to shape, the 'right mixture' of modernity and tradition. Again, they may or may not be in a position to influence deeply those in power or the larger social system. But many feel they could influence their immediate community including their organization and family.

What specific indications have led us to believe that Arab executives are ambivalent towards the old and the new? First, we shall briefly examine the types and sources of ambivalence within the executives' society. Later we will examine their feelings toward the West and especially the Western expatriates and businessmen.

The typical Arab executive we talked with is a proud person: he is proud of his nation and its people, and proud of his organization and its achievements. But invariably this executive is very aware of the weaknesses in his nation and its people. At times those interviewed would be depressed about the present conditions, and at times angry, but most of the time hopeful and desirous to rectify and improve the weak points. Most of these weaknesses have been examined within their contexts in the preceding chapters. It will be sufficient, therefore, to list the main ones, with a few words on the desired changes in each:

1. *Inter-Arab strife*: rectification of this may result in greater cooperation among Arab countries; political and economic stability; and a large common market with all its implications of growth and profits for executives.
2. *Low value of time*: any improvement would lead to better utilization of valuable (and often scarce) human resources. (This and the next point are especially relevant to governmental agencies).
3. *Lack of industrial mentality*: intensive industrial training and education may develop the desperately needed industrial

discipline and organizational skills among the work force and middle management.

4. *Extremes in 'informality' and 'personalism'*: the key phrase is striking a 'happy medium' between the extremes of the Arab style of 'informality' and 'personalism' in interpersonal relations, on the one hand, and the Western formal and impersonal style on the other. The likely outcome of such moderation will be improved efficiency while still retaining effectiveness in human relations.

Turning to the Arab executives' opinions of expatriates and/or foreign businessmen, we find not surprisingly that the characteristics which Arabs admire are the same ones they would like to see learned by their own people. The following are the characteristics most admired by the executives (figures in parentheses are frequencies of mention).

1. High value and respect for time (18)
2. Productivity and hard work (15)
3. Technical know-how and competence (10)
4. Organized and systematic approach to work (10)
5. Dedication and conscientiousness to work (9)
6. Discipline (5)
7. Accuracy and precision (5)

These, then, are the business-related characteristics which executives long for and which they miss most in their people. Yet these characteristics can be learned and acquired by employees and managers without giving up cherished values and institutions such as friendship, religion, family and the like. Clearly these characteristics have to be inculcated through life-time education (socialization): starting from childhood, in schools and universities, throughout work careers, to retirement. However, from the executives' viewpoint, training and education are never too late. Indeed, a few of the executives cited Japan as an example of a country in which the industrial mentality was instilled without drastic changes to its customs or traditions. While Arab and Japanese societies differ in many aspects and their circumstances are vastly different, Japan is nevertheless a reference 'model' to the Arab executive's mind of how modernization can be achieved in their own society while still retaining its distinctive Arab identity and character.

When the executives were asked to mention the characteristics of expatriates or foreign businessmen which they strongly dislike, there were two such characteristics which pertain to our topic.[31] The first relates to treatment of employees. Eleven executives strongly disliked the expatriates' manner of treating local employees, using the following terms to describe it: 'ruthless', 'treat like machines', 'inhumane', and 'easy resort to firing'. It is not difficult to understand the reasons for such resentment if we take into account on the one hand the expatriates' strong preoccupation with efficiency and productivity, and on the other hand the executives' paternalistic (and often emotional) management style. The second strongly disliked characteristic concerns what was seen by executives as the extremism in the 'business is business' approach. This approach was considered by nine Arab executives as too dry and impersonal for their part of the world.[32]

Once again, the crucial questions here are whether or not the industrial mentality could be acquired without sacrificing the desirable elements of Arab personality (such as hospitality, friendship, family-orientation, religiousness and so on)? Is the typical executive being realistic in holding these hopes and aspirations? Finally, at the macro-level, will societies and their institutions be able to maintain a 'mixture' of the traditional and modern? Clearly there are no easy answers to these questions. Yet they are the burning questions in the minds of all persons associated with change in the Arab world: politicians, businessmen, academics, and the like. Their own personal exposure to the West, and the subsequent changes in their own personality, have led many of them to believe that a mixture of the traditional and modern is indeed feasible.

NOTES

1. Hall, (1959), *The Silent Language*; Kluckhohn and Strodtbeck (1961), *Variations in Value Orientations*; McClelland (1961), *The Achieving Society*; Farmer and Richman (1965), *Comparative Management and Economic Progress*; and Robock, Simmonds, and Zwick (1977), *International Business and Multinational Enterprises*.
2. Kent (1969), *Corporate Financial Management*, p. 293.
3. See Patai (1973), *The Arab Mind*, pp. 147-50, 310. For critiques of this view see Rodinson (1974), *Islam and Capitalism*, English edn, chapter 4.

Also see Naim (1978), 'Towards a Demystification of Arab Social Reality', pp. 48-62.
4. Owen (1976), 'Islam and Capitalism: A Critique of Rodinson', p. 86. See also Mansfield (1976), *The Arabs*, pp. 95-105, for an analysis of the conditions of peasants.
5. Owen (1976), p. 86.
6. See Rodinson (1974), chapter 4, for a large number of such quotes.
7. See Patai (1973), p. 148, for a large number of quotes.
8. *The Quran*, Sūra XIII: 11 (A. Y. Ali's translation).
9. Compare this behaviour to the Christian Scientists' attitudes toward medical treatment.
10. *Time Magazine*, Europe Edition, 9 October, 1978, p. 8.
11. Similar to the finding of Y. Sayigh that political conditions constituted the greatest unknown facing the entrepreneurs which he surveyed in Lebanon in the early 1960s; Sayigh (1962), *Entrepreneurs of Lebanon*, p. 117.
12. It is interesting to note (Table 7.4) that six executives viewed good labour and employee relations as a preventive measure.
13. A strict interpretation of the Quran would result in condemnation of insurance; and in the Arab world only Saudi Arabia interprets it thus. However, insurance companies can operate in Saudi Arabia if they are registered elsewhere. *The Times*, 'Easy marriage of pragmatism and principle', a special report on *Insurance in the Arab World*, 27 November, 1978, p. II.
14. Radcliffe-Brown (1957), *A Natural Science of Society*, p. 87, as quoted in Nisbet (1972), *Social Change*, pp. 14-15. The first type of change is called 'readjustment change'; the second 'change of type'.
15. As has been suggested by many writers on modernization; see, for example, Lerner (1958), *The Passing of Traditional Society*; Kerr et al. (1960), *Industrialism and Industrial Man*; Levy (1965), *Modernization and the Structure of Societies*; Parsons (1966), *Societies: Evolutionary and Comparative Perspectives*; and Inkeles and Smith (1974), *Becoming Modern*.
16. Eisenstadt (1977), 'Convergence and Divergence of Modern and Modernizing Societies', p. 4; and Lauer (1971), 'The Scientific Legitimation of Fallacy', pp. 881-9.
17. Riggs (1964), *Administration in Developing Countries: The Theory of Prismatic Society*; and Riggs (1966), *Thailand: The Modernization of Traditional Polity*.
18. On Lebanon, see Khalaf and Shwayri (1966), 'Family Firms and Industrial Development'; and Farsoun (1970), 'Family Structure and Society in Modern Lebanon'. On Nigeria, see Ogionwo (1969), 'The Adoption of Technological Innovations in Nigeria', Ph.D. Thesis, University of Leeds; and Onyemelukwe (1973), *Men and Management in Contemporary Africa*. On Indonesia, see Geertz (1963), *Peddlers and Princes*.
19. Shaker (1972), 'Modernization of the Developing Nations: The Case of Saudi Arabia', Ph.D. diss., Purdue University, p. 383.
20. For criticisms of the 'convergence' school, see Desai (ed.), (1971), *Modernization of Underdeveloped Societies*, 2 vols, Eisenstadt (1973), *Tradition, Change, and Modernity*; Eisenstadt (1977); and Coser (1975), 'Structure and Conflict'.

21. Gusfield (1978), 'Review Essay', p. 446.
22. Shaker (1972) p. 383.
23. 'The Assertion of Islam', a leading article by *The Times* newspaper, London, 16 November, 1978. In Egypt, there has been a strong resurgence of Muslim fundamentalism, particularly among university students, young people, and labour union leaders. In fact, the labour union leaders have recently submitted to the Egyptian government a labour manifesto whereby the Constitution and the Islamic *Sharī'a* shall be the main sources of the law. See *Al-Ummāl* (Cairo), published by the General Federation of Egyptian Trade Unions, 17 July 1978, pp. 7-8.
24. Here, neo-traditionalist suggests a new form rather than a revival of the old; it is used as in 'neo-colonialism' rather than in 'neo-classical'.
25. See Prothro and Diab (1974), *Changing Family Patterns in the Arab East*, pp. 206-7.
26. Compared with 46 per cent in the major industrialized nations (Source: UN, *Yearbook of Labour Statistics*, 1977). The lower percentage is, of course, due to several reasons, one of which is the low employment of women. Another reason is the high percentage (44 per cent) of population under 15 years of age, compared with 25 per cent in five major industrial countries. (Source: *Ibid.*)
27. The twenty-seven executives were from all six countries. No significant relationship was found between their attitudes on this social change and their age, social or educational background.
28. For an excellent discussion of ambivalence and how it is built into normative structures, see Merton (1976), *Sociological Ambivalence and Other Essays*.
29. Merton and Barber (1963), 'Sociological Ambivalence'.
30. Sharabi (1961), 'Political and Intellectual Attitudes of the Young Arab Generation'; also see van Nieuwenhuijze (1971), *Sociology of the Middle East*, pp. 187, 656-7; and Khalid (1977), 'The Sociocultural Determinants of Arab Diplomacy', pp. 131-4.
31. The other characteristics will be discussed in the final chapter when we examine the implications of this study for expatriates or foreign businessmen.
32. See Chapter 6, section entitled: 'A preference for "informality"', for further comments on the 'business is business' approach.

8 Conclusion and Implications

> This is not the end. It is not even the beginning of the end. But it is, perhaps, the end of the beginning.
>
> W. S. Churchill, 1874–1965
> Speech at the Mansion House,
> 10 November, 1942

In the preceding chapters we have explored many topics at different levels of analysis: societal, organizational and individual. The aim was to sketch a portrait of the Arab executive against the background of a changing social landscape.[1] It is time now to stand back, as it were, and survey the main themes of that landscape. Themes that kept insisting upon being dragged into many of the topics we have been discussing.

THE IMPORTANCE OF ENVIRONMENTAL FACTORS

Throughout this book, we have seen the pervasive influence of the environment on business conditions, on social behaviour and on the attitudes of the Arab executive. Our approach has been to view the executive as part of a business-oriented social system (that is his organization) which, in turn, is embedded in his wider environment. Again, this environment is made up of socio-cultural values and norms, and social structural elements (institutions, groups and sets of social relations and roles). In each of the preceding chapters we have witnessed how the environment (despite its diversity and variety) is influencing the thinking and behaviour of the Arab executive.

For example, earlier in this book we saw how the economic and political instability as well as the recent economic boom are affecting business conditions. Furthermore, we examined how the formal institutions and groups are superimposed on the more powerful family and friendship groups. As a result there is a strong incentive for the Arab executive to rely upon family and friendship ties (connections) in managing his business.

The executive's time and performance are also influenced by socio-cultural values and norms. One of the most serious problems for the executive was the low value placed on time by people around him. We also found that the executive's role in the community and organization is congruent with society's paternalistic and familial nature. The environmental influence was apparent in the executive's styles of decision making and conflict management. We discovered the strong influence of traditional consultation on decision-making styles, and how the authority structure outside the organization is reflected by the executive's attitudes towards conflict management.

The environmental influence was perhaps most prominent when the Arab executive's interpersonal style was examined. Here we found that social values and norms, as well as social structural elements, encourage the executive to use 'personalized' and 'informal' approaches when dealing with his employees and with people outside his organization. Finally, the economic development and the modernization processes which are now taking place in Arab countries are creating ambivalent feelings for the Arab executive.

In short, the environment has a great influence on the executive's thinking and behaviour. This is not to advocate societal or social structural determinism. On the contrary, throughout the book we have attempted to highlight the strain and tension experienced by the executive, and we have repeatedly emphasized the executive's role, not only as a target of social influence but also as an agent of social change. In fact, had we considered only one side of what is obviously at least a two-sided phenomenon, we would have been committing a serious error. Hence, our second theme: the role of the executive in social change.

THE EXECUTIVE AS A CHANGE AGENT

Although the Arab executive is constrained to a large extent by societal and social structure forces, it is clear that these forces are not immune from change. Values, norms, institutions, groups, roles and so on do indeed change. Even the Islamic *Sharī'a* (Sacred Law) is seen 'metaphorically as an organic

CONCLUSION AND IMPLICATIONS

creature, growing, developing and evolving; attached with a strong link of interdependence to its society, adapting to its needs, and changing with different circumstances'.[2]

Arab executives can, and often do, play an important role in this social change. They may do that consciously or unconsciously, and they may also do it for self-interests or community interests. Whatever their motives, we have seen that the executives are indeed agents of social change in several of the topics we have discussed. For example, some executives are minimizing the fusion of their business, social, and personal lives – trying to separate or compartmentalize these main aspects of their lives. Other executives are actively discouraging the traditional open-door policy by insisting that their employees go through the organizational hierarchy. Still others are attempting to overcome the barriers to better utilization of time. Finally, nearly all executives are encouraging the use of highly sophisticated equipment and machinery within their organizations.[3]

There is, however, one area worthy of special mention to which some Arab executives felt they could increase their present contribution, namely, education.[4] Here education is used in the broadest sense of the word to include acquisition of knowledge and skills, especially managerial and vocational skills. Development of human resources is a never ending process and the executives, as employers and members of society, take over this heavy responsibility where the schools and universities leave off.

Finally, as change agents, Arab executives are bound to influence the process of modernization which is now taking place in Arab countries. The nature of this emerging modernization is the concern of our third theme.

MODERNIZATION WITHOUT SACRIFICING TRADITIONS

With modernization and the concomitant use of science and technology, it is very likely that Arab society will lose some of its traditional ways. Most Arabs, including our executives, would welcome the loss of certain characteristics which they perceive as obstacles to progress. For instance, the low value of time, poor organizational and work habits and the dislike of manual work. The predicament for the Arabs, however, is how to preserve their society's specifically Arab identity or character; also how to avoid the potential ills which often accompany extensive industrialization such as alienation and anomie;[5] emotional and spiritual decadence;[6] and other related problems which for many social scientists have marked the decline or end of ideology in post-industrial societies.[7]

In the preceding chapter, we have discussed various aspects of the intricate modernization process. The plausibility of a 'mixture' of the traditional and modern was suggested; and the ambivalent feelings of executives towards the old and new were discussed. We have also pointed out that there are no easy answers to the perplexing questions posed by modernization. There is, however, one thought worth emphasizing, namely, that social change can have both positive and negative aspects for the members of a given society, as so many social scientists have observed.[8] More specifically, that social change when pushed too rapidly may result in a negative backlash, especially if traditional values and norms are threatened.[9]

Clearly it is difficult to ascertain what the future holds for the Arab world. Social changes are not uniform in all parts of the Arab world, and are not likely to be so in the near future. Various ideologies exist (see Chapter 2) which range from secular to non-secular, from rightist to leftist, and so on – all searching for an *Arab* ideology. Most Arab political leaders, businessmen, academics and the like, would probably agree with the following conclusions reached by a writer on Arab history and contemporary affairs:

> No one can tell what political and social institutions the Arab people will have developed by the end of this momentous century. All that can be said with certainty is that, however much they derive from foreign movements and ideas, they will have a specifically Arab and Islamic character.[10]

IMPLICATIONS

Throughout this study the author has attempted, whenever feasible, to point out the implications of the findings for the several parties to whom this study may be of interst. The parties

CONCLUSION AND IMPLICATIONS 117

include: the Arab executive himself; his Arab employees; expatriates and foreign businessmen; management consultants and teachers; and finally social scientists and researchers. Many of the implications were clear and self-explanatory; spelling them out here would simply lead to lengthy recapitulation. There are, however, three important subjects for which the implications of this study must be explicitly emphasized and discussed:

I.   management training and development;
II. expatriate employees and foreign businessmen;
III. future research.

1. Management Training and Development

Before we discuss the implications of this study for training and development of Arab managers, we must examine briefly the current debate on what constitutes 'management principles' and whether these are transferable across nations.

For the past twenty years, management teachers and researchers have been engaged in a debate over the extent to which Western (usually American) management principles, practices and knowhow are exportable to other cultures.[11] Although there seems to be some agreement about what functions are performed by managers and organizations, there is disagreement about the skills, styles and techniques needed for performing these functions. The managerial functions are usually defined as the basic 'classical' ones of planning, organizing, controlling and directing (some management writers include other activities such as staffing, coordinating, and so on).[12] It is also agreed that business organizations appear to differentiate their activities by their specialized functions such as production, marketing, finance, personnel, and so on.

The debate, however, is mainly due to questions such as these: what constitutes 'good' management principles and practices? What about the recent contingency (situational) theories? Do we really know enough about the management process within a given culture to justify exporting it to other cultures? And if so, do we know enough about these other cultures to enable us to judge which management practices are applicable and which are not? These, then, are the issues which are likely to keep the above debate topical and lively.

The findings of this study strongly suggest that certain managerial styles and skills required in the Arab world may differ from those advocated or practised in Western cultures. Let us look at some of the practices which may not be applicable in most Arab organizations.

1. Joint decision making (or participative leadership style) is unlikely to be widely adopted by Arab managements, even for decisions which are best suited for this style. The major reasons for this are: (a) subordinates might view it as a sign of weakness on part of the executive: they expect to be consulted, but not to make the final decision; (b) Arab executives prefer and feel more at ease with the consultative decision-making style; and (c) Arab executives and subordinates tend to dislike team-work.
2. Conflict resolution and problem-solving techniques which rely on open confrontation such as T-Groups or Managerial Grid are unlikely to succeed in Arab organizations. Most Arabs are very sensitive to criticism, open confrontation, directness, and frankness especially when in front of a group. Deference to authority, face-saving, manliness, pride and loyalty – all of these act as serious obstacles to open confrontation.
3. Personnel selection or promotion based only on efficiency or achievement may frequently be violated in view of the importance in the Arab world of nepotism, loyalty, and personal connections.
4. Impersonal and formal systems or styles would be at a great disadvantage in an organizational and societal environment which is more person-oriented than task or role-oriented. The paternalistic nature of management would also discourage formality and impersonality.
5. Certain quantitative management systems or decision-making techniques (for example, Operational Research) which rely on stable or advanced infrastructures are often not usable. The business, economic, and governmental infrastructures in the Arab world are not well developed yet. Accurate information and data are scarce; manpower and materials are not easily available; governmental laws and regulations are unstable (changing on short notice); and governmental red tape is widespread. Executives often rely on intuition, 'gut feelings', or connections to get things done.

CONCLUSION AND IMPLICATIONS

Indeed some of the Western managerial practices may not only be inapplicable but may also be harmful if applied without adaptation to Arab environments. This would apply particularly to those managerial practices which deal with the personal aspects of management (points 1 to 4, above).

What, then, is needed for the training and development of Arab executives? There are at least five managerial skills which the present author feels can be beneficial to the development of present and especially future Arab executives.

1. *Conceptual skills.* The conceptual skills encourage the executive to see the 'whole' picture in terms of its detail. We have suggested earlier the analogy of the executive as a radar scanning his environment, and the increased use of the 'helicopter view' both of which increase the sensitivity to the complex processes in a fast-changing environment. The conceptual skills would lead to improved corporate policies and strategies which are in keeping with Arab environments.
2. *Delegation.* By more frequent use of delegation the executive can (a) save his time; (b) train his employees; (c) utilize his employees' existing skills and resources; and (d) motivate his employees. We have discussed this issue in Chapter 4 where the findings indicated a low level of delegation.
3. *Conflict management.* In Chapter 5 we suggested that executives should encourage opposition (devil's advocate and so on) from subordinates. Training can help the executive change his own attitudes, as well as his employees' expectations, towards 'reasonable and constructive' opposition.
4. *Management of time.* The management of time in the Arab business world is as much a management of social relations problem as it is proper utilization of one's working hours. Time is precious but it has many competing factors (Chapter 7) which constrain and complicate management of time. Skills must be learnt to deal with both facets of this problem.
5. *Change agent skills.* Earlier in this chapter we discussed the role of the executive as an agent of change. Skills appropriate to this role would include skills of introducing change, managing resistance to change, and understanding the process of change and its consequences.

These five skills have been selected for special emphasis because of their relevance to the findings of this study. Clearly, there are many other managerial skills and functions of equal significance ranging from leadership or human relations skills to the functional skills in marketing or finance.

II. Expatriate Employees and Foreign Businessmen

A deeper understanding of the Arab executive and his environment can be extremely beneficial to expatriates and foreign businessmen. The cost of failure to adjust to a new culture or the cost of business mistakes can be very high for non-Arabs wishing to work in or with Arab organizations. The need for cooperation between Arabs and non-Arabs is mutual. There is a great shortage of skilled manpower in the oil-producing countries; and the huge oil wealth has created trade and business opportunities in the whole region for both Arab and foreign enterprises.

Although the scope of the present study did not include the examination of problems facing expatriates/foreign businessmen who are engaged in business in the Arab world, it did, however, examine the attitudes of a few expatriates towards the Arab executive, and also the attitudes of the Arab executive towards expatriates/foreign businessmen. This was done mainly to increase our understanding of the Arab executive, but it has also provided information which may have important implications for expatriates/foreign businessmen.

This information helps the non-Arab in two ways. First, by understanding the Arab executive (and the environmental elements which influence him), the non-Arab should be able to reduce the culture shock which is so often experienced by people interacting with members of a society different from their own. This should speed the adaptation and adjustment process, and is likely to yield benefits to both the Arab and non-Arab. A second way of reducing the cultural barrier would be for the non-Arab to receive feedback about his own image as perceived by Arab executives. This study provides some feedback. It was accomplished by asking Arab executives which characteristics they admired most and which they strongly disliked about expatriates/foreign businessmen. Most of the responses were presented in the various sections of the previous two chapters. Let us now summarize these responses in Table 8.1. The strongly disliked characteristic of arrogance and sense

TABLE 8.1 The image of expatriates/foreign businessmen as perceived by Arab executives

Most admired characteristics*	Frequency of mention†	Strongly disliked characteristics	Frequency of mention†
1. High value and respect for time	18	1. Arrogance and sense of superiority	21
2. Productivity and hard work	15	2. Inability or unwillingness to understand or respect local traditions/mentality	15
3. Technical know-how and competence	10		
4. Organized and systematic approach to work	10	3. 'Inhumane' treatment of employees	11
5. Dedication and conscientiousness to work	9	4. Extremism in 'business is business' approach	9
6. Discipline	5	5. Money-orientation only	6
7. Accuracy and precision	5		

* As presented and discussed in Chapter 7.
† Characteristics mentioned by five or more executives.

of superiority warrants a brief remark. There are at least three possible explanations for this image: (1) the behaviour of non-Arabs toward Arabs is actually arrogant; (2) the behaviour seems to be arrogant to some Arabs because they feel they are lacking in certain skills; or (3) the non-Arab's behaviour is so impersonal and formal that it unintentionally conveys arrogance. Of course, it is likely that a combination of these explanations is at work here.[13] The investigation of this characteristic, and all the others shown in Table 8.1, is clearly an important future research project, which of course must take into account not only the Arab executive's perceptions but also those held by the expatriates and foreign businessmen.

Finally, the findings presented in this study are merely a start to the necessary and valuable cross-cultural training for expatriates (and their spouses) as well as foreign businessmen wishing to work in the Arab world.

III. Future Research

The approach used in this study has influenced the suggestions for future research. Let us, therefore, briefly restate the reasoning behind this approach. The present study of the Arab executive has been exploratory. It has also avoided direct comparison of Arab executives with those from other societies. References to Western societies were occasionally made only to illuminate the topics under discussion. Thus the reader was encouraged to compare the Arabs with whichever society he is most familiar. There were two reasons for this type of approach. First, the dearth of systematic research on business and management in the Arab world encourages exploratory work and discourages premature comparison. Second, having examined most of the recent literature on cross-cultural research, the present author is persuaded that Karlene Roberts' conclusion, based on her critical review ten years ago of cross-cultural research, is still applicable today. Roberts concluded at that time that:

> Organizations are rarely viewed as parts of their environments, yet understanding organizational-environmental interactions seems a major practical reason for engaging in cross-cultural research.[14]

CONCLUSION AND IMPLICATIONS

Roberts went on to recommend that:

> ... more effort be invested in understanding behaviour in a *single culture*, developing middle-level theories to guide explorations, and seeking the *relevant questions* to ask across cultures (p. 347, emphasis added).

This study is only the beginning of the quest towards a better understanding of the Arab executive. Future research is direly needed into several areas of which the following seem to be the most urgent:

1. Following up, elaborating and testing the large number of hypotheses suggested by this study. Added emphasis must be placed on explaining the similarities and differences between executives from the various Arab countries.[15]
2. In order to complement the present findings, future research must focus on the expectations and attitudes of Arab employees at the middle and lower organizational levels.
3. Future studies of the adjustment and adaptation problems of expatriates working in the Arab world will add a new and different perspective to this subject. The results should be valuable both to expatriates and Arab executives.
4. As more empirical data on the behaviour and thinking of Arab executives and their employees become available, cross-cultural research will then become more feasible and meaningful.

The researcher, like the management consultant and teacher, must bear in mind the main findings of this book. These findings emphasized the strong links that exist between the Arab executive and his environment. Further, the researcher must become aware and sensitive to the fact that both the environment and members of Arab society are going through a critical period in their history. Indeed, the Arabs have now left the 1970s, their *decade of awareness*, and have entered the 1980s, their *decade of action* and rapid change.

NOTES

1. To use R. Nisbet's metaphors of the sociological portraits and landscapes; see Nisbet (1976), *Sociology as an Art Form*.

2. Yamani (1972), 'Islamic Law and Contemporary Issues', p. 53.
3. See especially Chapters 3, 6, and 7 for more examples.
4. Several large organizations have their own vocational training centres; in addition, as mentioned in Chapter 7, several companies pay for the university education of prospective managers.
5. Black (1966), *Dynamics of Modernization: A Study in Comparative History*, pp. 27–34.
6. Nisbet (1976), pp. 132–5.
7. Lipset (1976), 'Social Structure and Social Change', pp. 190–203.
8. Robock *et al.* (1977), *International Business and Multinational Enterprise*, p. 338.
9. Events in Pakistan, and more recently in Iran, support this observation.
10. Peter Mansfield (1976), *The Arabs*, p. 552.
11. Richman (1965), 'Significance of Cultural Variables', p. 292. See also Newman (1970), 'Is Management Exportable?'; and Evan (1976), *Organization Theory*, Chapter 15.
12. The 'classical' functions of management were introduced by Henri Fayol in 1916.
13. One expatriate felt that this arrogance has been reversed in some Arab countries in the past few years.
14. Roberts (1970), 'On Looking at an Elephant', p. 347.
15. At least one more North African country should be included in future studies, such as Algeria, Libya, Morocco, or Tunisia.

Appendix 1: Methodology and Data Analysis

METHODOLOGY

The fifty-two Arab executives interviewed for this study were purposefully selected to meet a number of requirements. First, they came from three non-oil exporting countries: Egypt, Jordan, and Lebanon; and from three oil-exporting countries: Kuwait, Saudi Arabia, and the United Arab Emirates. Second, an attempt was made to select executives from three organizational size categories: small (180–499 employees), medium (500–999 employees), and large (over 1000 employees). Third, from each country we attempted to select top executives from organizations whose nature of business was classified as follows: manufacturing; trade and services (many of these firms were in construction and contracting);[1] and conglomerate (firms with diversified activities, usually including manufacturing). For the other variables, see Table A.1.

Some of the executives were selected from *Major Companies of the Arab World*;[2] others were suggested by various chambers of commerce, friends, relatives, or business associates. In each country, the author typically began the field work with a list of fifteen to twenty executives of whom six to ten, depending on the country, were interviewed. The typical semi-structured interview lasted 1 hour and 20 minutes. The executives were given the choice of conducting the interview in either Arabic or English. About 40 per cent chose Arabic, 40 per cent English, and about 20 per cent used both languages. Most of the interviews took place in ten Arab cities (in six countries), but a few were conducted in London.

DATA ANALYSIS

Due to the exploratory nature of this study, most of the data collected were based on nominal- and ordinal-level scales. The simple χ^2 test was used on such data.

TABLE A.1 A statistical profile of Arab executives and their organizations

Country	N	Executives' age: mean (range)	University education				Social background			Status		Organizational size*				Organizational ownership			Nature of business		
			None	Arab	Western	Mixed	Tribal	Rural	Urban	Owner	Non-owner	Small	Medium	Large	Mean Size	Family	Partnership	Government	Mfg.	Trade and service	Conglomerate
Egypt	9	52 (40–62)	—	7	1	1	—	1	9	3	6	2	2	5	3561	3	—	6	7	2	—
Jordan	10	52 (39–69)	1	5	1	3	—	7	3	7	3	7	2	1	527	4	5	1	7	2	1
Kuwait	9	42 (33–52)	2	—	1	6	—	8	2	6	3	1	4	4	2457	7	1	1	1	5	3
Lebanon	8	44 (33–53)	1	5	1	1	—	4	4	4	4	4	2	2	2287	1	7	—	3	5	—
Saudi Arabia	10	42 (29–50)	2	—	2	6	1	4	5	6	4	2	2	6	1402	3	3	4	5	3	2
UAE	6	45 (38–53)	2	1	—	3	2	1	3	3	3	2	2	2	1872	2	4	—	1	4	1
Totals	52	46 (29–69)	8	18	6	20	3	25	24	29	23	18	14	20	2482	20	20	12	24	21	7

* Organizational size: Small = 180–499 employees; Medium = 500–999 employees; Large = over 1000 employees.

In Chapter 4, however, the power-sharing continuum (Figure 4.1) was defined and measured by a four-point equal interval scale. The equal interval assumption allowed us to use multiple regression and correlational techniques.

Interval Scale

The assumption of interval scale is consistent with assumptions made by other researchers. Thus, Heller,[3] using a similar continuum, assumed a five-point equal interval scale. While Vroom and Yetton[4] developed an ordered metric scale which resulted in equal intervals between their three major decision styles, excluding their two minor styles A11 and C11 (see Table 4.1). The values for the three major styles were: autocratic (A1)=0, consultative (C1)=5, and group decision (G11)=10; styles which closely correspond to our styles 1, 2, and 3. Vroom and Jago[5] have extended the Vroom and Yetton model to include individual problems and have, therefore, included delegation (D1) on their scale assigning a value of 10 to it. The present research assumes that delegation, Style 4, is also separated from Style 3 by an equal distance (see Figure 4.1).

Decisional categories

The seven decisions given to the executives were broken down into three categories: personnel, departmental, and organizational. This was based on the nature of the decisions as well as on the high intercorrelation between the decisions within each category. For example, the first three decisions were highly interrelated, and were not consistently related to any other category of decisions (see Figure A.1).

Multiple regression analysis

Some of the independent variables were interrelated.[6] To control for any spurious relationships and to isolate only those variables which contribute substantially to the variation in decision-making styles, multiple regression statistical technique was used.

First, dummy variables were created in order to dichotomize the nominal-scale variables and to incorporate them in the parametric analyses. Second, Pearson product–moment corre-

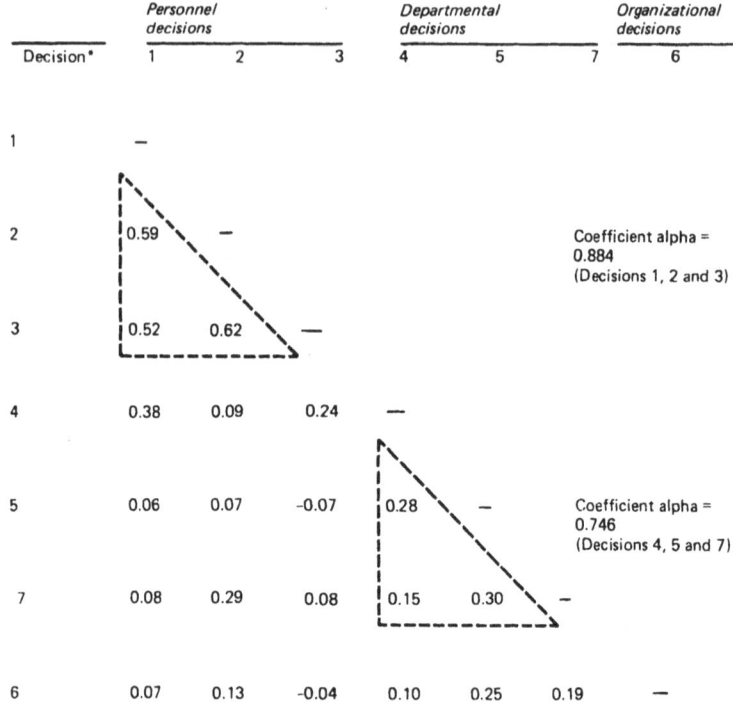

FIGURE A.1 Pearson correlation matrix (7 decisions)

* For details of decisions 1 to 7, see Interview Schedule, Appendix 2, or Chapter 4.

lation coefficients were calculated between all independent variables and the three categories of decisions (the dependent variables). This gave us zero-order correlations. Next, partial correlation methods provided us with first-order and second-order correlations. Finally, variables were retained in the regression equation if their marginal contribution to the proportion of the variance accounted for was significantly greater than zero, all other variables being controlled.

Table A.2 illustrates the calculations of the amount of variance explained by the independent variables for the organizational decision category (Decision 6). The significant contributions came from the first and second variables only; accounting for 20.31 per cent of the variance in decisional style (for Decision 6). The same procedure as above was used for the other two decisional categories; see Table 4.6.

TABLE A.2 Analysis of variance (organizational decision 6)

Independent variable	Explained sums of squares	Unexplained sums of squares	AR^2	F ratio	df	Significance
1. Lebanon	146.94	—	9.55	6.38	1,50	0.025
2. No university education	304.25	993.82	10.76	7.76	1,49	0.01
3. Kuwait	358.05	940.03	2.75	2.75	1,48	N.S.

AR^2 is the adjusted square of multiple correlation coefficient. It is adjusted for the number of independent variables in the equation and the number of cases.
N.S. = not significant.

NOTES

1. Organizations whose business was restricted to management of banks, hospitals, and hotels were not included.
2. *Major Companies of the Arab World*, Graham and Trotman Ltd., London, 1977.
3. Heller (1971), *Managerial Decison-Making*, p. 53.
4. Vroom and Yetton (1973), *Leadership and Decision-Making*, pp. 65–71.
5. Vroom and Jago (1974), 'Decision Making as a Social Process', pp. 743–69.
6. The intercorrelations were not high enough to cause problems of multicollinearity. The highest correlation among independent variables was 0.46.

Appendix 2: The Interview Schedule

THE ARAB EXECUTIVE

This research work is intended for the doctorate degree in business management, University of London. Personal interviews are needed with senior Arab executives in several Arab countries. Each interview will cover the following topics:

I. General information
II. The executive and his environment
III. Decision making
IV. Interpersonal relations
V. Attitude towards time and change

Your personal help would be deeply appreciated. It would also contribute to the advancement of knowledge on this subject.

Farid A. Muna

I. General information

Code number: ....

Nature of business: ....
Location of head office: ....
Principal countries of operation: ....
Total number of employees: ....
Number of other Arabs: .... Non-Arabs: ....
Age of company: .... Type of ownership: ....
How long have you been with the company?: ....
Present position: .... How long in this position?: ....
To whom do you report (if applicable)?: ....
Number of managers reporting directly to you: ....
Previous positions with this organization: *Duration*
....
....
....

                       Where   *Positions*   *Duration*
Other work experience: ....
....
....

                       Where   *Public or Private*
Education: High School ....
                       Where   *Degree*   *Subject*
     College or University ....
....
                 Who ran courses   *Subject*   *Duration*
Training courses: ....
....

Languages: ....
Age: .... Place of birth: .... Nationality: ....
In which place did you spend most of your *first* 18 years of life?: ....
Marital status: .... Wife's nationality: ....
Is she a close relative?: ....
No. of children: .... Age range: ....

APPENDIX 2: THE INTERVIEW SCHEDULE 133

No. of children:............ Age range:...
How would you describe your relations with your extended family?:...
....
Outside activities (hobbies, clubs, groups, etc.):.......................
....

II. The Executive and His Environment

1. What are the main business activities, duties or responsibilities on which you find yourself spending most of your time (in and out of the organization)?:

   Approx. % of time

   ....
   ....
   ....
   ....

2. When making the following decisions what are the main factors you would take into consideration:
   (a) Hiring a national manager:
   (a manager at the lowest level you would normally be concerned with)
   (b) Hiring a non-national manager: Other Arabs...............
   Non-Arabs.................

3. In your community (social and business circles) who are the one or two persons whose thoughts and opinions you respect most highly? Why? (No names needed, only role or social status):

4. Do you ever consult persons/groups from outside your firm when making business decisions? If so, whom, under what circumstances and why?

5. Because of your high position in this company, what are some of the things that are expected of you by:
   (a) people in your community?:
   (b) top people in government?:
   (c) your extended family?:
   (d) your employees?:

6. Could you please mention some of the ideas, programmes, or changes that you as an executive would like to implement, but find yourself restricted from doing so because of Arab traditions, customs, and values (in and out of the organization):

APPENDIX 2: THE INTERVIEW SCHEDULE 135

7. Do you find that your work and your position as a senior executive influence your family life or your community life? How and in what ways? Please, give some examples:

8. When making serious *personal* decisions individuals often ask themselves: 'What would *people* think or say if I do this or that?' If and when this happens to you, could you please rank in the order of importance the type of people you would have in mind:

9. How do you perceive your role as a senior executive both inside and outside your company?:

10. What do you consider to be the main problems or obstacles which you, as a senior executive in the Arab world, are facing at the present time (with examples)?

III. Decision making

Decision making can be considered as a prime factor in management. In fact, some writers go to the extent of defining management and decision making as synonymous terms. There are, however, many ways and methods in which business decisions are made. Rarely is there one perfect method that can be applied to all decisions in all situations. Below are four alternative methods that apply to relations with subordinates:

I. The decision is made by you, no consultation or discussion with subordinate(s).
II. Prior consultation with subordinate(s); he/they may or may not influence your final decision.
III. You and your subordinate(s) *together* analyse the problem and come to a decision – subordinates have as much influence as you have on the final (majority) decision.
IV. Ask subordinate(s) to make decision on his/their own.

The above possible alternatives can be applied not only to subordinates, but also to colleagues, superiors, and others (both in and out of the organization). Please indicate which of these alternatives you would normally use to arrive at the following decisions:

1. The decision to promote one of the employees directly supervised by one of your subordinates.
2. The decision to discipline one of the employees directly supervised by one of your subordinates.
3. The decision to terminate the services of one of the employees directly supervised by one of your subordinates.
4. The decision to reduce the total workforce by 20 per cent.
5. The decision to increase the workforce in a subordinate's department/division.
6. The decision to introduce a new product/enter a new market/take on a new project/expand existing work facilities.
7. The decision to alter/modify the formal organization chart (changes in job and/or responsibilities, re-organization) in your subordinate's department/division.

In your role as a senior Arab executive, you may occasionally be called upon to deal with disagreements between yourself and a person reporting directly to you. Could you please tell me how you have handled such disagreements in the past. For example, let us suppose that you and one of your staff completely disagree about the promotion of a key employee working for him. Please indicate how you would in the end deal with this conflict:

(a) When you favour it and he opposes it:
(b) You oppose it and he favours it:

As a second example, let us suppose that you and one of the employees who reports directly to you completely disagree about an expansion plan (or a new product or a new project) which involves and affects his department/division. Please indicate how you would in the end deal with this conflict:

(a) When you favour it and he opposes it:
(b) You oppose it and he favours it:

Finally, can you think of proverbs or sayings (in Arabic or English) which guide you or influence your thinking when handling these types of disagreement?

IV. Interpersonal Relations

1. In your own community, to what extent do people rely on family ties, friendships or other means of influence to get things done, or done faster? Examples, please.

   Do you feel that this is a help or a hindrance to you in the performance of your duties as a senior Arab executive? Examples, please:

2. When would you use *formal* methods of getting business done within the Company, and why?:

   When would you use *informal* methods of getting business done within the Company, and why?:

3. Let us suppose that a foreign friend of yours wants to do business in this country; what would you tell him about our customs and practices regarding the giving and taking of gifts and other acts of reciprocity, especially how these practices are used in business?:

4. The ideal employee would be, among other things, *both* loyal and efficient. But, unfortunately, this does not always occur. In such cases, then, which would you prefer to have, *employees* in your company who are:
   (a) more loyal to the company?:.....................................
   (b) more efficient on the job?:.......................................

   What about your preference concerning your own immediate subordinate... Would you prefer your *immediate subordinate* to be:
   (a) more loyal to you?:..
   (b) more efficient in his work?:.....................................

5. During the past few weeks or so, please think of the employees who have asked, and were able to contact you or have a meeting (interview) with you. Do they belong to:
   ____ Any level of the company (without going through hierarchy)?

APPENDIX 2: THE INTERVIEW SCHEDULE 139

____ Any level, provided they go through proper hierarchy (channels)?
____ Managerial level only?
____ Immediate subordinates only?

6. How often do you personally give instructions to employees at the middle or lower levels without going through their immediate supervisors?:
____ Very often
____ Occasionally
____ Seldom

7. (a) When starting a business discussion, would you normally spend a period of time offering greetings, refreshments, and social talk of a general nature?:

   (b) In which situations and with whom would you do this?:

   (c) Do you feel that this custom is beneficial or is it mostly a waste of time? Why?

8. What are some of the characteristics of the expatriates employed here (if no expatriates, then foreign businessmen) which you admire most? Why?

   What about characteristics which you strongly dislike? Why?

9. What are some of the managerial practices of foreign businessmen working in the major industrial nations which you believe can be learned and then applied to your business here? Why?

10. If you were to describe the personal traits and characteristics that contributed to your success, which would be the most important ones?:

V. Attitude Towards Time and Change

1. What are the most common reasons which occasionally cause you to be late to:
   A business meeting or appointment?:
   A social occasion (lunch, dinner)?:

2. What proverb or saying would best represent your views and attitudes towards time (in Arabic or English)?:

3. Please indicate on the scale below which period of time best describes your expectations when undertaking the following:

   (a) Payback on capital investment

Under 1 yr.	1-2 yr.	3-5 yr.	6-10 yr.	Over 10 yr.

   (b) Company-wide planning

Under 1 yr.	1-2 yr.	3-5 yr.	6-10 yr.	Over 10 yr.

   (c) Looking ahead in managerial training and development

Under 1 yr.	1-2 yr.	3-5 yr.	6-10 yr.	Over 10 yr.

4. Could you please name some of the happenings that have had a direct effect on your business, but over which you have had little control:

5. Do you ever take steps or measures to prevent undesirable events from occurring? Examples, please?

6. Do you carry life insurance?   ____ Yes   ____ No
   If not, why not?

7. Change and innovation in the Arab world are phenomena which are fairly easy for a person to see and feel. In your position as a senior executive, where do you get your ideas about changes and innovations which you feel can be introduced in your company? Please name these sources of ideas:

APPENDIX 2: THE INTERVIEW SCHEDULE

8. How do you feel about the following changes?:

   (a) Women holding high managerial positions in business firms.

Do you:	Strongly favour	Favour	Oppose	Strongly oppose

   Likelihood of it happening in the next 5–10 years:

Very likely	Likely	Not likely	Highly unlikely

   (b) An increase in the introduction of sophisticated scientific systems and equipment to business (computers, latest machinery, etc.) when and where applicable.

Do You:	Strongly favour	Favour	Oppose	Strongly oppose

   Likelihood of it happening in the next 5–10 years:

Very likely	Likely	Not likely	Highly unlikely

   (c) The newer generation to gain more freedom and independence from family, customs, religion, and traditions. (For example, a move from the extended family to the nuclear one and so on.)

Do you:	Strongly favour	Favour	Oppose	Strongly oppose

   Likelihood of it happening in the next 5–10 years:

Very likely	Likely	Not likely	Highly unlikely

9. Before we end this interview (we have indeed covered many topics and subjects) is there anything else you would like to discuss, or voice an opinion on, which is related to this subject?

Bibliography

Ali, Abdullah Yusuf (1975), *The Holy Qur'ān: Text, Translation and Commentary* (The Muslim Students' Association of the USA and Canada).

Antoun, R. T. (1965), 'Conservatism and Change in the Village Community: A Jordanian Case Study', *Human Organization*, 24, pp. 1-10.

Al-Awaji, Ibrahim M. (1971), 'Bureaucracy and Society in Saudi Arabia', Ph.D. dissertation, University of Virginia.

Ayoub, Victor F. (1965), 'Conflict Resolution and Social Reorganization in a Lebanese Village', *Human Organization*, 24, pp. 11-17.

Badre, A. Y. and Siksek S. G. (1960), *Manpower and Oil in Arab Countries* (Beirut: American University of Beirut).

Barnard, Chester I. (1938), *The Functions of the Executive* (Cambridge, Mass.: Harvard University Press).

Berger, Morroe (1957), *Bureaucracy and Society in Modern Egypt: A Study of the Higher Civil Service* (Princeton, NJ: Princeton University Press).

—— (1962), *The Arab World Today* (London: Weidenfeld & Nicolson).

Bill, James and Leiden, Carl (1974), *The Middle East, Politics and Power* (Boston: Allyn & Bacon).

Black, C. E. (1966), *Dynamics of Modernization: A Study in Comparative History* (New York: Harper & Row).

Blau, Peter M. (1964), *Exchange and Power in Social Life* (New York: Wiley).

—— (1976), 'Parameters of Social Structure', in P. M. Blau (ed.) *Approaches to the Study of Social Structure* (London: Open Books).

Cartwright, D. (1965), 'Influence, Leadership and Control', in J. G. March (ed.) *Handbook of Organizations* (Chicago: Rand McNally).

Casadio, Gian Pablo (1976), *The Economic Challenge of the Arabs* (London: Saxon House/D. C. Heath).

Central Statistical Office (1979), *Financial Statistics* (London: HMSO). (March).

Coon, Carleton S. (1958), *Caravan: The Story of the Middle East* (rev. ed.) (New York: Holt).

Coser, L. A. (1956), *The Functions of Social Conflict* (New York: Free Press).

—— (1976), 'Structure and Conflict' in P. M. Blau (ed.) *Approaches to the Study of Social Structure* (London: Open Books).

Dahl, R. A. (1957), 'The Concept of Power', *Behavioural Science*, 2, pp. 201-8.

Desai, A. R. (ed.) (1971), *Modernization of Underdeveloped Societies*, 2 vols. (Bombay: Thacker).

Eisenstadt, S. N. (1964), 'Social Change, Differentiation and Evolution' in L. Coser and B. Rosenberg (eds.), *Sociological Theory: A Book of Readings*, 4th ed. (New York: Macmillan, 1976).

—— (1973), *Tradition, Change and Modernity* (New York: Wiley).

—— (1977), 'Convergence and Divergence of Modern and Modernizing Societies: Indications from the Analysis of the Structure of Social Hier-

archies in Middle Eastern Societies', *International Journal of Middle Eastern Affairs*, 8, pp. 1-27.
Eliot, T. S., 'Burnt Norton', *Four Quartets* (London: Faber & Faber, 1944) ll. 1-3.
Europa Publications (1978), *The World of Learning, 1978-79*, vols. 1 and 2 (London).
Evan, William M. (1976), *Organization Theory* (New York: Wiley).
Farmer, R. and Richman, B. (1965), *Comparative Management and Economic Progress* (Homewood, Ill.: Irwin).
Farsoun, Samih K. (1970), 'Family Structure and Society in Modern Lebanon' in Louise E. Sweet (ed.), *Peoples and Cultures of the Middle East*, vol. 2 (Garden City, New York: The Natural History Press).
Fayerweather, John (1960), *Management of International Operations* (New York: McGraw-Hill).
Fiedler, F. E. (1967), *A Theory of Leadership Effectiveness* (New York: McGraw-Hill).
French, J. R. P., Jr., and Raven, B. H. (1959), 'The Bases of Social Power' in D. Cartwright (ed.), *Studies in Social Power* (Ann Arbor, Mich.: Institute of Social Research).
Geertz, Clifford (1963), *Peddlers and Princes: Social Development and Economic Change in Two Indonesian Towns* (Chicago: University of Chicago Press).
Goldthorpe, J. E. (1975), *The Sociology of the Third World* (Cambridge: Cambridge University Press).
Graham & Trotman Ltd. (1977), *Major Companies of the Arab World* (London).
Gulick, John (1976), *The Middle East: An Anthropological Perspective* (Pacific Palisades, California: Goodyear).
Gusfield, J. R. (1978), 'Review Essay', *American Journal of Sociology*, 82, No. 2, pp. 443-8.
Hall, Edward T. (1959), *The Silent Language* (New York: Doubleday).
—— and Whyte, W. F. (1960), 'Intercultural Communication: A Guide to Men of Action', *Human Organization*, 19, No. 1, pp. 5-12.
Hall, J. (1971), 'Decisions, Decisions, Decisions', *Psychology Today*, 5 (November).
Hazen, William E. and Mughisuddin, Mohammed (1975), *Middle Eastern Subcultures* (Lexington, Mass.: D. C. Heath).
Heidenheimer, A. J. (1971), *Political Corruption: Readings in Comparative Analysis* (New York: Holt, Rinehart & Winston).
Heller, Frank A. (1971), *Managerial Decision-Making* (London: Tavistock).
Hitti, Philip K. (1970), *History of the Arabs*, 10th edn. (London: Macmillan).
—— (1971a) *Islam: A Way of Life* (London: Oxford University Press).
—— (1971b) *The Arabs: A Short History* (London: Macmillan).
Hobday, Peter (1978), *Saudi Arabia Today* (London: Macmillan).
Homans, George C. (1961), *Social Behaviour* (New York: Harcourt).
Hourani, Albert (1962), *Arabic Thought in the Liberal Age, 1798-1939* (London: Oxford University Press).
Inkeles, Alex and Smith, David H. (1974), *Becoming Modern: Individual Changes in Six Developing Countries* (Cambridge, Mass.: Harvard University Press).

Jabra, Jabra I. (1971), 'Arab Language and Culture' in Michael Adams (ed.) *The Middle East: A Handbook* (New York: Praeger).
Jacoby, N. H., Nehemkis, P., and Eells, R. (1977), *Bribery and Extortion in World Business* (New York: Macmillan).
Katz, Daniel and Kahn, Robert L. (1978), *The Social Psychology of Organizations*, 2nd ed. (New York: Wiley).
Kelman, H. C. (1958), 'Compliance, Identification and Internalization: Three Processes of Attitude Change', *Journal of Conflict Resolution*, 2, pp. 51–60.
Kent, Raymond (1969), *Corporate Financial Management*, 3rd edn. (Homewood, Ill.: Irwin).
Kerr, C., Dunlop, J., Harbison, F. and Meyers, C. (1960), *Industrialism and Industrial Man* (Cambridge, Mass.: Harvard University Press).
Khalaf, S. and Shwayri, Emile (1966), 'Family Firms and Industrial Development: The Lebanese Case', *Economic Development and Cultural Change*, 15 (October), pp. 59–69.
Khalid, Mansour (1977), 'The Sociocultural Determinants of Arab Diplomacy' in G. N. Atiyeh (ed.) *Arab and American Cultures* (Washington D.C.: American Enterprise Institute for Public Policy Research).
Kluckhohn, F. and Strodbeck, F. (1961), *Variations in Value Orientation* (New York: Row, Peterson).
Lauer, Robert H. (1971), 'The Scientific Legitimation of Fallacy: Neutralizing Social Change Theory', *American Sociological Review*, 36, pp. 881–9.
Lerner, Daniel (1958), *The Passing of Traditional Society: Modernizing the Middle East* (Glencoe, Ill.: Free Press).
Levy, M. J. (1965), *Modernization and the Structure of Societies: A Setting for International Affairs* (Princeton, N.J.: Princeton University Press).
Lewin, Kurt; Lippitt, Ronald; and White, Robert K. (1939), 'Patterns of Aggressive Behaviour in Experimentally Created Social Climates', *Journal of Social Psychology*, 10, pp. 271–99.
Lewis, Bernard (1970), *The Arabs in History*, 5th edn. (London: Hutchinson).
Likert, R. (1967), *The Human Organization* (New York: McGraw-Hill).
Lipset, Seymour Martin (1976), 'Social Structure and Social Change' in P. M. Blau (ed.), *Approaches to the Study of Social Structure* (London: Open Books).
Mabro, Robert and Radwan, Samir (1976), *The Industrialization of Egypt, 1939–1973* (Oxford: Oxford University Press).
MacDonald, Robert W. (1965), *The League of Arab States: A Study in the Dynamics of Regional Organization* (Princeton, N.J.: Princeton University Press).
Maier, N. R. F. (1955), *Psychology in Industry*, 2nd edn. (Boston: Houghton-Mifflin).
Mann, F. C. (1964), 'Toward an Understanding of the Leadership Role in Formal Organizations', in R. Dubin, G. Homans and D. Millar (eds.) *Leadership and Productivity* (San Francisco: Chandler).
Mansfield, Peter (1976), *The Arabs* (London: Allen Lane).
McClelland, D. (1961), *The Achieving Society* (Princeton, N.J.: Van Nostrand).
MEIRC, S.A. (1975), 'Attitude Survey of Saudi and Kuwaiti Employees', unpublished report, Beirut, Lebanon.

MEIRC, S.A. (1976a), 'Job Attitude Survey of Omani National Staff', July 1976, unpublished report, Beirut, Lebanon.
—— (1976b), 'Das Island Attitude and Motivation Survey', September 1976, unpublished report, Beirut, Lebanon.
—— (1976c), 'Labour and Social Insurance Regulations: Saudi Arabia', Law Division, November 25, 1976, unpublished report, Beirut, Lebanon.
—— (1977), 'A Summary Analysis of the Labor Movement in the Middle East and North Africa', January 1977, unpublished report, Athens, Greece.
—— (1978), 'A Summary Analysis of the Labor Movement in the Middle East and North Africa', January 1978, unpublished report, Athens, Greece.
Melikian, Levon H. (1977), 'The Modal Personality of Saudi College Students: A Study in National Character', in L. C. Brown and N. Itzkowitz (eds.), *Psychological Dimensions of Near Eastern Studies* (Princeton, N.J.: Darwin Press).
—— and Diab, Lutfy N. (1959), 'Group Affiliations of University Students in the Arab Middle East', *Journal of Social Psychology*, 49, pp. 145-59.
—— ——, (1974), 'Stability and Change in Group Affiliations of University Students in the Arab Middle East', *Journal of Social Psychology*, 93, pp. 13-21.
Merton, Robert K. (1976), *Sociological Ambivalence and Other Essays* (New York: Free Press).
—— and Barber, E. (1963), 'Sociological Ambivalence', in E. A. Tiryakian (ed.), *Sociological Theory, Values, and Sociocultural Change* (New York: Free Press).
Middle East Economic Survey 'Atiqi on Investment in Arab World' (7 November, 1977), Vol. XXI, No. 3, pp. i-vi.
Mills, C. Wright (1959), *The Sociological Imagination* (New York: Oxford University Press).
Mintzberg, Henry (1973), *The Nature of Managerial Work* (New York: Harper & Row).
—— (1973), 'The Manager's Job: Folklore and Fact', *Harvard Business Review*, July-August, pp. 49-61.
Moore, W. E. (1969), 'Social Structure and Behaviour', in G. Lindzey and E. Aronson (eds.), *The Handbook of Social Psychology* (2nd edn.), vol. 4 (Reading, Mass.: Addison Wesley).
Morris, Desmond (1967), *The Naked Ape* (New York: McGraw-Hill).
Muna, Farid A. (1979), 'The Arab Executive Mind', Ph.D. thesis, University of London.
Naim, Samir (1978), 'Towards a Demystification of Arab Social Reality', *Review of Middle East Studies*, No. 3 (London: Ithaca Press).
Newman, W. H. (1970), 'Is Management Exportable?', *Columbia Journal of World Business*, Jan.-Feb. 1970.
Nieuwenhuijze, C. A. O. van (1971), *Sociology of the Middle East* (Leiden: Brill).
Nightingale, Donald (1976), 'Conflict and Conflict Resolution', in George Strauss *et al.* (eds.), *Organizational Behaviour* (Belmont, California: Wadsworth).
Nisbet, Robert (ed.) (1972), *Social Change* (Oxford: Basil Blackwell).
—— (1976), *Sociology as an Art Form* (London: Heinemann).

Nuseibeh, Hazam Z. (1956), *The Ideas of Arab Nationalism* (Ithaca, N.Y.: Cornell University Press).
Nutting, Anthony (1964), *The Arabs* (New York: Mentor, The New American Library).
Ogionwo, W. W. (1969), 'The Adoption of Technological Innovations in Nigeria: A Study of Factors Associated with Adoption of Farm Practices', Ph.D. thesis, University of Leeds.
Onyemelukwe, C. C. (1973), *Men and Management in Contemporary Africa* (London: Longman).
Owen, Roger (1976), 'Islam and Capitalism: A Critique of Rodinson', *Review of Middle East Studies*, No. 2 (London: Ithaca Press).
Parsons, Talcott (1966), *Societies: Evolutionary and Comparative Perspectives* (Englewood Cliffs, N.J.: Prentice-Hall).
Patai, Raphael (1973), *The Arab Mind* (New York: Scribners).
Prothro, E. Terry and Diab, Lutfy N. (1974), *Changing Family Patterns in the Arab East* (Beirut: American University of Beirut).
Radcliffe-Brown, A. R. (1940), 'On Social Structure', *Journal of the Royal Anthropological Institute*, 70, pp. 1–12.
—— (1957), *A Natural Science of Society* (New York: Free Press).
Richman, B. M. (1965), 'Significance of Cultural Variables', *Academy of Management Journal*, 8, No. 4.
Riggs, Fred W. (1964), *Administration in Developing Countries: The Theory of Prismatic Society* (Boston: Houghton Mifflin).
—— (1966), *Thailand: The Modernization of Traditional Polity* (Honolulu: University Press of Hawaii).
Roberts, Karlene H. (1970), 'On Looking At an Elephant: An Evaluation of Cross-Cultural Research Related to Organizations', *Psychological Bulletin*, 74, No. 4 (November 1970).
Robock, S., Simmonds, K. and Zwick, J. (1977), *International Business and Multinational Enterprises* (rev. edn.), (Homewood, Ill.: Irwin).
Rodinson, Maxime (1974), *Islam and Capitalism*, English edn. (Harmondsworth, Middlesex: Penguin).
Sampson, Anthony (1975), *The Seven Sisters* (London: Hodder & Stoughton).
—— (1977), *The Arms Bazaar* (London: Hodder & Stoughton).
Sayigh, Yusif (1962), *Entrepreneurs of Lebanon* (Cambridge, Mass.: Harvard University Press).
Shaker, Fatina Amin (1972), 'Modernization of the Developing Nations: The Case of Saudi Arabia', Ph.D. dissertation, Purdue University.
Sharabi, Hisham B. (1961), 'Political and Intellectual Attitudes of the Young Arab Generation', in Tibor Kerekes (ed.), *The Arab Middle East and Muslim Africa* (New York: Praeger).
—— (1966), *Nationalism and Revolution in the Arab World* (New York: Van Nostrand Reinhold).
Simon, Herbert A. (1957), *Administrative Behavior* (New York: Macmillan).
Stinchcombe, Arthur L. (1965), 'Social Structure and Organizations', in J. G. March (ed.), *Handbook of Organizations* (Chicago: Rand McNally).
Tannenbaum, R. and Schmidt, W. H. (1958), 'How to Choose a Leadership Pattern', *Harvard Business Review*, 36, pp. 95–101.
Thomas, J. M. and Bennis, W. G. (eds.) (1972), *Management of Change and Conflict* (London: Penguin Books).

Thomas, K. (1976), 'Conflict and Conflict Management', in M. D. Dunnette, (ed.), *Handbook of Industrial and Organizational Psychology* (Chicago: Rand McNally).
—— and Walton, R. E. (1971), 'Conflict-Handling Behaviour in Interdepartmental Relations', Research Paper No. 38, Graduate School of Business Administration, University of California, Los Angeles.
Tomeh, Aida K. (1970), 'Reference-Group Supports Among Middle Eastern College Students', *Journal of Marriage and the Family*, 32, pp. 156–65.
United Nations (1977), *Yearbook of Labour Statistics* (New York).
—— (1978), *Demographic Yearbook* (New York).
Vroom, Victor (1976), 'Leadership', in M. D. Dunnette (ed.), *Handbook of Industrial and Organizational Psychology* (Chicago: Rand McNally).
—— and Jago, A. G. (1974), 'Decision Making as a Social Process: Normative and Descriptive Models of Leader Behavior', *Decision Sciences*, 5, pp. 743–69.
—— and Yetton, Philip (1973), *Leadership and Decision-Making* (Pittsburgh: University of Pittsburgh Press).
Weber, Max (1947), *The Theory of Social and Economic Organization* (Oxford: Oxford University Press).
Yamani, Ahmed Zaki (1972), 'Islamic Law and Contemporary Issues' in Charles Malik (ed.), *God and Man in Contemporary Islamic Thought* (Beirut: American University of Beirut).

MAGAZINES AND NEWSPAPERS:
Al-Ahrām (Cairo), 15 January 1978.
Alam Attijarat, vol. 13, No. 2 (London), February 1978.
Al-Bilād (Riyadh), 15 October 1976.
The Financial Times (London), 18 December 1978; 26 February 1979.
Time Magazine, Europe edition, 9 October 1978.
The Times, (London), 12 June 1978; 16 and 27 November 1978.
Al-Ummāl (Cairo), 17 July 1978.

Index

Abassid empire, 7-8
Agent of change, Arab executive as, 1, 33, 42, 82, 91, 98, 114-15, 119
Al-Ahrām, 62n, 147
Alam Attijarat, 43n, 147
Algeria, 10, 14, 25n, 124n
Ali, Abdullah Yusuf, 70n, 111n, 142
Ambivalence, 1, 4, 67-8, 104, 106-10, 114
American University of Beirut, 10, 36, 61n, 107
Amman Stock Exchange, 9
Antoun, R. T., 43n, 142
Arab
  identity, 1, 5-7, 109, 116, see also History; Arabic language; Religion
  nationalism, 13-15
  socialism, 10, 14
  unity, 14-15
Arab Labour Organization (ALO), 22-3
Arab League, 6, 8
Arab Maritime Petroleum Transport Company, 19
Arab Petroleum Investments Corporation, 19
Arab Petroleum Services Company, 19
Arab Shipbuilding & Repair Yard Company, 19
Arab-Israeli conflict, 14, 16-18
Arabic language, as a basis of identity, 5-7
Al-Atiqi, Abd al-Rahman, 16
Authority, deference to, 70n, 118
Al-Awaji, Ibrahim M., 87n, 142
Ayoub, Victor F., 70n, 142
Al-Azhar University, 24n

Badre, A. Y., 25n, 142
Bahrain, 25n

Barber, E., 112n, 145
Barnard, Chester I., 61n, 142
Beirut Stock Exchange, 9
Bennis, W. G., 70n, 146
Berger, Morroe, 23-4n, 86n, 142
Al-Bilād, 25n, 147
Bill, James, 13, 24n, 142
Black, C. E., 124n, 142
Blau, Peter M., 24n, 86n, 142
Bribery, 76-8
Buqra (tomorrow) attitude, 29
Business agents, see Middlemen
Business is Business' attitude, 85-6, 110, 112n

Capital investment, see Time horizons
Cartwright, D., 61n, 142
Casadio, Gian Pablo, 25n, 142
Change
  agent, see Agent of change
  attitudes towards, 88, 98-110
  social, 86, 98, 102-6, 116
  technological, 98, 102-6
  types of, 99-100, 111n
Classical managerial functions, 117, 124n
Commercial and industrial tradition, 5, 8-9
Communication, 82
Community, types of social communities, 11, 13, see also Social structure
Comparative management, 3, 122
Conceptual skills, 38, 119
Conflict
  dyadic, 63-4, 68
  management of, 1, 4, 63-9, 114, 118-19
  proverbs on, 64, 68-9
  role of third party (mediator), 63, 65
  see also Power tactics

149

Confrontation, as taboo, 63, 65, 69, 118
Connections, 22, 37-8, 71, 74-8, 83, 114, 118
  bribery, 76-8
  corruption, 76-7
  reciprocity, 75-8
Consultation, 36, 49, 58-60, 63, 85, 114
  as a tactic for conflict reduction, 59, 65, 68-9
  in decision making, see Decision-making styles
  reasons for, 59-60
Contacts, see Connections
Contingency approach, 45, 53, 58, 61-2n, 117
Coon, Carleton, S., 24n, 142
Corruption, 76-7
Coser, L. A., 70n, 142
Cross-cultural research, 3, 98, 117, 122-3
Cultural bias, 4n
Culture, 27, see also Socio-cultural values and norms
Culture shock, 21, 83, 120

Dahl, R. A., 61n, 142
Decision-making
  departmental decisions, 51-2, 54-8, 127
  organizational decisions, 52, 55, 57-8, 127-9
  personnel decisions, 51, 53-5, 58, 127
  socio-psychological variables affecting, 52-8
  variables affecting, 45, 53-8
Decision-making profile, 47-53
Decision-making styles, 1, 4, 44-50, 53-61 passim, 85, 114, 127
  consultative, 46-50, 58, 118, 127
  delegation, 45-50, 58, 127
  joint decision (democratic), 46-50, 58, 60, 118. 127
  own decision (autocratic) 45-50, 58, 127
Delegation
  advantages of, 45, 47, 61, 119
  and decision making, see decision-making styles
  low levels of, 60-1, 91
Desai, A. R., 111n, 142
Diab, Lutfy N., 24n, 35, 43n, 112n, 145-6
Differentiation
  partial, 12-13, 84, 100
  social and economic, 11-13, 99

Economic
  boom, 14, 18-23, 45, 113, 120
  developments, 4, 5, 13, 18-23
  infrastructure, 19, 21, 23, 91, 118
  instability, 21, 23, 92, 97, 108, 113, 118
Economically active population, 105, 112n
Eells, R., 144
Egypt, 3, 7, 10, 14, 25n, 50-3, 55-7, 62n, 86n, 101, 103-4, 112n, 125-6
Eisenstadt, S. N., 24n, 111n, 142
Eliot, T. S., 88, 143
Environment
  importance of environmental factors, 113-14, 120
  sensitivity to, 38-9, 119 123
Evan, William M., 124n, 143
Executive role in the organization
  chief executive role, 39-40
  family role, 40-1
Expatriates, 3, 20-1, 71, 83-6, 86-7n, 89, 107-10, 112n, 124n
  image of, 120-2
  implications for, 4, 117, 120-2
  see also Culture shock, and 'Business is Business' attitude
Expectations, of Arab executives and employees,
  see Role of executive
  see also Self-fulfilling prophecy
Extended Family, see Family

Face-saving, 60, 118
Faisal, King of Saudi Arabia, 16, 87n, 101
Familial, see Paternalistic
Family
  expectations of, 1, 36-7

extended family, 11, 33, 35-6, 42, 91
freedom from family and traditions, 102-6
importance of, 11-13, 22, 35-7, 71, 74-5
Farmer, R., 110n, 143
Farsoun, Samih K., 24n, 43n, 70n, 86n, 111n, 143
Fatalism
myth of, 4, 93-8
and preventive measures, 96-8
and uncontrollable events, 97-8
Fayerweather, John, 78, 87n, 143
Fayol, H., 124n
Fiedler, F. E., 61n, 143
Foreign businessmen, *see* Expatriates
Formal system, *see* Informality
French, J. R. P., Jr., 61n, 70n, 143
Friendship ties, 12-13, 22, 74-5, 90, 114
Future, attitudes towards the, *see* Change; *see also* Time

Geertz, Clifford, 111n, 143
Gifts and bribery, 77-8
Goldthorpe, J. E., 24n, 143
Governmental bureaucracy, 22, 108, 118
development plans, 19, 92-3
laws and regulations, 21, 118
Group
affiliation and interaction, 12, 36
patterns, 12, 113
reference groups, 31
role of small groups, 12-13, 113
Gulick, John, 24n, 43n, 143
Gusfield, J. R., 112n, 143

Ḥadīth, 59, 95
Hall, Edward T., 73, 86n, 110n, 143
Hall, J., 70n, 143
Harbison, F., 144
Hayward, H. C., 25n
Hazen, William E., 25n, 143
Heidenheimer, A. J., 87n, 143
Helicopter view, 38, 119, *see also* Conceptual skills
Heller, Frank A., 45-7, 52, 61n, 127, 130n, 143

Hierarchy
downward bypassing, 82-3
upward bypassing, 81-2, 115
see also Open-door tradition
History of the Arabs, as a basis of identity, 5-7
Hitti, Philip K., 2, 9, 23-4n, 70n, 143
Hobday, Peter, 87n, 143
Homans, George C., 86n, 143
Hospitality, 11, 33, 77, 90
Hourani, Albert, 7, 143

Ijmā', 23n
Impersonal, *see* Person-oriented
Individual variables
age of executive, 41, 52-8, 79, 126
education, 10, 41, 52-8, 79-80, 126
social background, 11, 52-8, 79, 126
status in organization, 9, 52-8, 79-80, 126
Indonesia, 25n, 100
Industrialization, potential ills of, 116
Informality, 4, 13, 60, 71, 83-6, 109, 114, 118
Inkeles, Alex, 111n, 143
Inshā' Allāh, 96
Insurance, life, 98, 111n
Inter-Arab conflict, 8, 14-15, 17, 108
Intermediary role, 36-8, 43n, 75, 86n
International Confederation of Arab Trade unions (ICATU), 22
International Labour organization (ILO), 22-3
Interpersonal styles, 1, 4, 71-86 *passim*, 91, 114
Interview Schedule, 4, 68, 70n, 131-41
Iran, 25n, 101, 124n
Iraq, 10, 14, 18, 25n
Islam, 6-8, 15-16, 59, 94-6, 101
Islamic fundamentalism, 15-16, 112n
Israel, *see* Arab-Israeli conflict

Jabra, Jabra I., 23n, 144

Jacoby, N. H., 86n, 143, 144
Jago, A. G., 61n, 127, 130n, 147
Japan, 36, 101, 109
Jordan, 3, 14, 17, 25n, 29, 33, 50–3, 103–4, 125–6

Kahn, Robert L., 38, 43n, 69–70n, 144
Katz, Daniel, 38, 43n, 69–70n, 144
Kelman, H. C., 70n, 144
Kent, Raymond, 110n, 144
Kerr, C., 111n, 144
Khalaf, S., 111n, 144
Khalid, Mansour, 112n, 144
Kinship, *see* Family
Kluckhohn, F., 110n, 144
Kuwait, 3, 14, 16, 25n, 33–4, 50–2, 98, 100, 103–4, 125–6, 129
Kuwait Stock Exchange, 9

Labour unions, 14, 22–3, 25n
Lauer, Robert H., 111n, 144
Leadership styles, 44, 61n, 118, *see also* Decision-making styles
Lebanon, 3, 17, 33, 50–2, 55, 57, 86n, 100, 103–4, 125–6, 129
Leiden, Carl, 13, 24n, 142
Lerner, Daniel, 111n, 144
Level of analysis, 3–4, 26, 113
Levy, M. J., 111n, 144
Lewin, Kurt, 47, 144
Lewis, Bernard, 24n, 144
Libya, 23n, 25n, 124n
Likert, R., 47, 144
Lippitt, Ronald, 47, 144
Lipset, Seymour Martin, 124n, 144
Loyalty
    and efficiency, 79–80, 83
    importance of, 11, 71, 78–80, 118

Mabro, Robert, 62n, 144
McClelland, D., 110n, 144
MacDonald, Robert W., 23n, 144
Maier, N. R. F., 47, 144
Majlis, 81, 87n
Managerial Grid, 118
Managerial training and development, *see* Time horizons
Mann, F. C., 43n, 144
Manpower
    shortage, 19–20, 45, 105, 120
    supply, 18, 25n
Mansfield, Peter, 111n, 124n, 144
MEIRC, S. A., 25n, 43n, 144–5
    research studies by, 41–2
Melikian, Levon H., 24n, 43n, 70n, 145
Merton, Robert K., 112n, 145
Meyers, C., 144
Middle East Economic Survey, 25n, 145
Middlemen (business agents), 8, 76–7
Mills, C. Wright, 5, 145
Mintzberg, Henry, 38, 42–3n, 61n, 145
Modernity – *see* Modernization
Modernization, 1, 4, 16, 35, 37, 88, 98, 100–2, 106–10, 114, 115–16
Moore, W. E., 24n, 145
Morocco, 23n, 124n
Morris, Desmond, 73, 86n, 145
Motivation, *see* Delegation
Mu'āwiyah, the Caliph, 63, 68–9
Mughisuddin, Mohammed, 25n, 143
Muhammad, the Prophet, 7–8, 23n, 59
Multiple regression analysis, 53, 127–9
Muna, Farid A., 4n, 47, 131, 145
Muslim, *see* Islam

Nai'f, Prince of Saudi Arabia, 16, 25n
Naim, Samir, 111n, 145
National employee
    side-business opportunities for, 22
    training of, 37, 42, 108–9, 115, 119
Nationalism, *see* Arab nationalism
Nehemkis, P., 144
Newman, W. H., 124n, 145
Nieuwenhuijze, C. A. O. van, 23–4n, 112n, 145
Nigeria, 25n, 100
Nightingale, Donald, 69n, 145
Nisbet, Robert, 111n, 123–4n, 145
Non-decision making, as a power tactic, 65–6, 69
Norms, *see* Socio-cultural values and norms

INDEX

Nuseibeh, Hazem Z., 23n, 146
Nutting, Anthony, 23n, 146

Ogionwo, W. W., 111n, 146
Oil, *see* Petroleum
Oman, 25n
Onyemelukwe, C. C., 111n, 146
Open-door tradition, 71, 80-3, 91, 115
Organization of Arab Petroleum Exporting Countries (OAPEC), 19, 24-5n
Organization of Petroleum Exporting Countries (OPEC), 18, 25n
Organizational structure, 68, 81, 83-5
Organizational variables
country, 3, 52-8, 79, 125-6
nature of business, 52-8, 79
ownership, 3, 40, 52-8, 79, 125-6
size, 3, 40, 52-8, 61, 62n, 79, 125-6
see also Individual variables
Organized chaos, 84
Ottoman Turks, 7, 14
Owen, Roger, 111n, 146

Pakistan, 101, 124n
Palestine, *see* Arab-Israeli conflict
Parsons, Talcott, 87n, 111n, 146
Participation, 46-7, 118
Patai, Raphael, 110-11n, 146
Paternalistic, 1, 40-2, 45, 78, 80, 85, 110, 114, 118
Personal ties, 71, 74-8, 83, 90
Personalism, *see* Person-oriented
Personalized, *see* Person-oriented
Personnel selection, 80, 118
Person-oriented, 4, 13, 60, 71, 73-4, 80, 83, 86, 91, 109, 114, 118
Petroleum, discovery of, 9, 14, 18
Planning, *see* Time horizons
Political
developments, 4, 5, 13-18
instability, 14, 23, 92, 97, 108, 113
Power
in conflict management, 63-9
position, 65-6
tactics, 4, 65-6, 69
Power-sharing, 4, 44-5, 51, 64

continuum, 45, 47, 50, 127
see also Decision-making styles
Pride, 11, 118
Prothro, E. Terry, 24n, 35, 43n, 112n, 146

Qatar, 25n
Qiyās, 23n
Quran, Holy, 8, 23n, 44, 59, 68-9, 95, 111n

Radcliffe-Brown, A. R., 24n, 111n, 146
Radwan, Samir, 62n, 144
Raven, B. H., 61n, 70n, 143
Religion, as a basis of identity, 5-7
Research
future, 4, 28, 67, 106, 117, 122-3
methodology, 4, 125
Richman, B. M., 110n, 124n, 143, 146
Riggs, Fred W., 12, 24n, 84, 87n, 100, 111n, 146
Rituals, in conducting business, 71-4, 86n, 91
Roberts, Karlene H., 122-3, 124n, 146
Robock, S., 110n, 124n, 146
Rodinson, Maxime, 24n, 94-5, 110-11n, 146
Role of executive
in community, 1, 4, 26, 35-9, 42, 74, 91, 114
in organization, 1, 4, 26, 39-42, 81, 91, 114
see also Executive role in the organization
Role-oriented, 73, 80, 83, 118
Rural, 11-13, 78

Sampson, Anthony, 25n, 87n, 146
Saudi Arabia, 3, 7, 14-16, 18, 20, 25n, 29-30, 33, 50-2, 55-7, 84, 98, 100-1, 102-4, 111n, 125-6
Sayigh, Yusif, 111n, 146
Schmidt, W. H., 47, 146
Self-fulfilling prophecy, 41-2
Shaker, Fatina Amin, 111-12n, 146
Sharabi, Hisham B., 24n, 112n, 146
Sharī'a, 7, 15-16, 23n, 112n, 114

Sharjah Group Company, 9, 24n
Shūra, 59
Shwayri, Emile, 111n, 144
Siksek, S. G., 25n, 142
Simmonds, K., 110n, 146
Simon, Herbert A., 61n, 146
Smith, David H., 111n, 143
Social exchange, *see* Connections
Social influence, Arab executive as *agent* and *target* of, 26, 34, 42, 44, 98, 114
 see also Agent of change
Social pressures, 26-34, 42, 44, 75, 91
 dislike of manual work, 28, 30, 34, 115
 fusion of business, social and personal, 28, 30-1, 34, 91, 115
 high expectations for success, 28, 33-4
 individualistic approach to work, 28-30
 industrial mentality, 28-9, 34, 108-9, 115
 low value of time, 28-9, 34, *see also* Time
 marketing constraints, 28, 30
 nepotism, 28, 33-4, 78, 80, 118
 reputation in community, 28, 31-2
 restrictions on women, 28-9, 34, 42n, 102-3, 105
 social visits at the office, 28, 32-4, 91
 top-man syndrome, 28, 32, 91
 weekend problem, 28, 30
Social responsibility, 37
Social structure, 1-3, 5, 10-13, 24n, 71, 74, 78, 86, 99-100, 113-14
Socio-cultural pressures, *see* Social pressures
Socio-cultural values and norms, 1, 4, 11, 27, 34, 42, 69, 78, 80, 86, 99, 108, 113-14
Stinchcombe, Arthur L., 24n, 146
Strodbeck, F., 110n, 144
Subordinates
 bypassing, 81-3
 compliance by, 67
 opposition from, 63-9, 119
Sunna, 23n

Sūra, 59
Syria, 10, 14, 25n
System, business-oriented social, 2, 26, 60, 113

Tannenbaum, R., 47, 146
T-Groups, 118
The Financial Times, 24-5n, 147
The Times, 43n, 111-12n, 147
Thomas, J. M., 70n, 146
Thomas, K., 69-70n, 147
Time
 attitudes towards, 4, 88-98
 constraints on, 26, 31, 42, 44, 72-4, 76, 90-1, 119
 management of, 47, 91, 115, 119
 proverbs on value of, 89-90
 value of, 1, 89-91, 108, 114-15
Time horizons
 capital investment, 91-3, 96
 corporate planning, 91-3, 96
 managerial training and development, 91-3, 96, 108-9, 115
Time Magazine, 111n, 147
Tomeh, Aida K., 24n, 43n, 147
Traditions
 neo-traditionalist, 102, 112n
 sacrificing, 16, 101, 104, 109-10, 115-16
Training and development of Arab executives, 4, 39, 93, 117-20
 harmful Western managerial practices, 118-19
 managerial skills, 119-20
Tribal, 11-13, 78
Tunisia, 14, 124n

Umayyad empire, 7, 68
Al-Ummāl, 112n, 147
United Arab Emirates, 3, 25n, 30, 50-2, 85, 89, 100, 103-4, 125-6
United Nations, 23n, 112n, 147
Urban, 11-13, 78

Values, *see* Socio-cultural values and norms
Vroom, Victor, 45, 47, 53, 61n, 127, 130n, 147

Walton, R. E., 70n, 147
Wastah, 43n, *see also* Connections
Weber, Max, 61n, 147
White, Robert K., 47, 144
Whyte, W. F., 73, 86n, 143
Women
 in management, 102-6
 restrictions on 28-9, 34, 42n, 102-3, 105

Yamani, Sheikh Ahmed Zaki, 15-16, 25n, 124n, 147
Yetton, Philip, 45, 47, 53, 127, 130n, 147

Zwick, J., 110n, 146

GPSR Compliance

The European Union's (EU) General Product Safety Regulation (GPSR) is a set of rules that requires consumer products to be safe and our obligations to ensure this.

If you have any concerns about our products, you can contact us on

ProductSafety@springernature.com

In case Publisher is established outside the EU, the EU authorized representative is:

Springer Nature Customer Service Center GmbH
Europaplatz 3
69115 Heidelberg, Germany

www.ingramcontent.com/pod-product-compliance
Lightning Source LLC
Chambersburg PA
CBHW031521100426

42873CB00013B/164